A CONCISE HISTORY OF *The Spanish Civil War*

A CONCISE HISTORY OF

The Spanish Civil War

GABRIEL JACKSON

with 156 illustrations

THAMES AND HUDSON

For Dee

Frontispiece: Though executed under the impact
of the Peninsular War, Goya's work graphically
expresses the conflicts and violence that have
marked Spanish history in the nineteenth and
twentieth centuries. In this painting, entitled
Fight With Clubs, two men exchange blows,
oblivious of the quicksands that threaten to
engulf them.

Picture research: Georgina Bruckner

© 1974 Thames and Hudson Ltd, London

First paperback edition 1980
Reprinted 1982

Printed and bound in Great Britain by
The Camelot Press Ltd, Southampton

CONTENTS

PREFACE

More than thirty years after the triumph of General Franco the Spanish Civil War remains fascinating and controversial both within Spain and internationally. There are several reasons for this: the background of intense ideological struggle; the coincidence of the war with the international confrontation of Fascism, Communism and Democracy; the occurrence of revolution and counter-revolution; the ferocity, the commitment and at times the nobility of the participants; and the permanent human interest of the spiritual issues involved. At the same time, the truth has not been easy to discover. The victors have used their powers of censorship to see that only their version has been published within Spain. The exiles have had to write without benefit of archives. No one, either among the participants writing their memoirs or among professional historians, has had access to all the relevant documents, and no one has been able to free himself entirely of emotional preferences.

For the general reader I should say that I have been studying the subject since 1950, have published numerous scholarly articles and reviews, and one long book, in the preparation of which I read everything I could lay hands on, spent a full year in Spain, and interviewed more than one hundred active participants from both camps. In the present book I have tried to summarize the best research and published work of the last thirty years. I have not tried to free myself of preferences for social democracy, and for complete religious and political toleration, preferences which throw my main sympathy to the defeated Republican forces. But I have striven to see the Nationalists as they saw themselves, and to write of them with respect. History is not a story of good guys versus bad guys, though it may be a story in the interpretation of which honest men have to agree to disagree.

Since this is a brief treatment without detailed scholarly apparatus, I wish to indicate the differences between it and my earlier writings. My personal research in primary sources has dealt with the cultural renaissance of the late nineteenth and early twentieth centuries, and with the political and economic history of the years 1931–36. When I wrote *The Spanish Republic and the Civil War, 1931–1939*, I was concerned with the optimistic beginnings, the hesitations and errors, and finally the military overthrow of the Republic. Within that framework the Civil War was seen as ending a hopeful political experiment which in turn had been the fruit of six decades of cultural and political progress under the constitutional monarchy. In the present work the focus is different. I am particularly concerned with the elements of revolution and counter-revolution, the international ramifications of the war, and the importance of the wartime Nationalist government as the forerunner of contemporary Spain.

Several graduate students working with me have contributed substantially to my knowledge of particular questions: José Alvarez Junco (anarchist attitudes during the prime ministership of Largo Caballero); Juan Pablo Fusi (peasant demands and violence); Rosa Rexach (circumstances surrounding the unification of the Falange in April 1937); Patricia Fouquet (the relation of Falange doctrine to European Fascism); and Joaquín Arango (the extent of provable Portuguese intervention). I owe important naval information to Juan García Duran of the Fondren Library at Rice University, Houston, Texas; and I have benefited greatly from the unpublished researches and the vigorous conversation of Professor William Watson of the Massachusetts Institute of Technology and Mr Herbert R. Southworth, probably the most knowledgeable living bibliographer of the Spanish Civil War. I am most grateful also for financial aid from the Committee on Research of the University of California, and for excellent typographic and cartographic aid from Mrs Pamella Jung and Mrs Eunice Konold of the Department of History.

Author's note to this paperback edition (1979)
The research of recent years has enabled us to estimate more accurately certain figures which must inevitably remain approximate. The figures to which I call attention are smaller than those I used in 1973. They are the numbers of casualties at Guernica (p. 124), the gold shipment to the Soviet Union (p. 152), the total deaths attributable to the Civil War (p. 175), and the reprisal deaths exacted by the victors (p. 176).

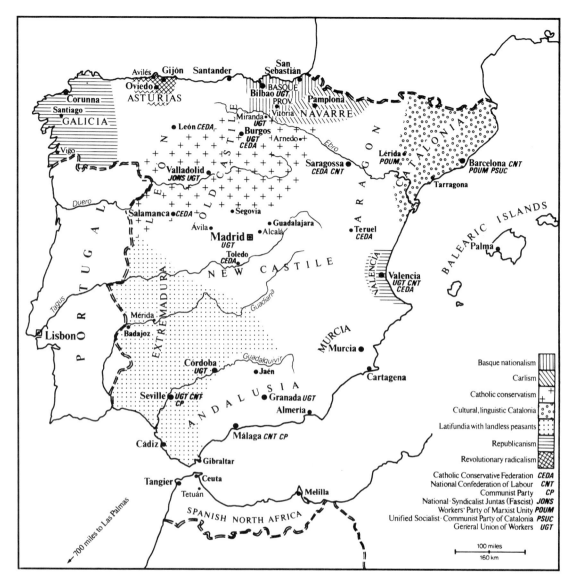

Regional political geography of pre-Civil War Spain, showing the areas of strength of the various political groupings.

Front page of an October 1902 issue of *El Liberal*, an 'enlightened' bourgeois newspaper published in Barcelona. The drawing, of the Festival of Our Lady of Mercy (revived as a popular *fiesta* in 1902), is by Picasso.

Chapter One

THE BACKGROUND OF THE
CIVIL WAR

In the year 1936 a fair proportion of Spaniards over fifty years of age could recall a time when life in their country had been relatively tranquil. In 1890 Spain had been neither as powerful nor as prosperous as Great Britain, France or Germany, but standards of living, and educational and economic opportunities, were noticeably improving. Politically the country seemed to be evolving toward limited monarchy, with effective executive power alternating between the civilian chieftains of the Conservative and Liberal parties. Electoral results outside the main cities were still being manufactured by the Minister of the Interior, but there was almost complete freedom of the press and sufficient freedom of political

May Day demonstration in Barcelona, by the late nineteenth century the chief industrial city of Spain and, after 1911, base of the anarcho-syndicalist National Confederation of Labor.

activity so that several Republican and regionalist parties, and a Socialist party, could organize, distribute literature, hold public meetings and present candidates in municipal and Cortes elections.

However, while the older generation might cherish memories of progress and tranquility, the great majority of Spaniards in 1936 had lived their entire lives in an atmosphere of instability and conflict. In the brief Spanish-American War of 1898, Spain had been forced to surrender the last remnants of her former world empire: Cuba, Puerto Rico and the Philippines. The humiliated army and navy felt that they had been betrayed by the civilian government, and their leaders became morbidly sensitive to public criticism. They resolved firmly to expand what they considered to be their civilizing and pacifying mission in North Africa, the nation's only remaining area of imperial activity; and they thought of themselves increasingly as the final guardians of order and tradition in the peninsula.

In 1906 the army demanded a Law of Jurisdictions which gave it the right to court-martial journalists who published disparaging articles about the military. In 1909 popular protests against sending

Down with the American eagle! An outburst of patriotic war fever in Spain during the 1898 war against the United States.

General Miguel Primo de Rivera and King Alfonso XIII (front row, first and second on the left), with members of the military directorate which ruled Spain from 1923 to 1930.

conscript soldiers to fight in Morocco touched off the 'Tragic Week' in Barcelona, in which 120 persons died, and 60 churches and government buildings were burned. In 1917 the army broke a Socialist-led railway strike. Between 1919 and 1923 the troubled industrial city of Barcelona was ruled essentially by martial law, with army generals in charge. In 1921 a military disaster in Morocco led to a parliamentary investigation, and when its embarrassing results were about to be published in 1923, King Alfonso XIII, in collaboration with the army, replaced the parliamentary monarchy with the dictatorship of General Miguel Primo de Rivera. When, by 1930, the dictatorship had lost its initial momentum, the King sacrificed Primo, attempted to maintain himself by means of two other brief

military cabinets, and then fled his country when the municipal elections of April 1931 indicated such widespread revulsion against the monarchy that no significant portion of the armed forces would offer to defend his throne. Yet barely sixteen months later a military hero of the Moroccan campaigns, General Sanjurjo, tried to overthrow the Republic on behalf of conservative and monarchist forces. Thus Spaniards living in 1936 would automatically anticipate army intervention on the conservative side of any grave social conflict.

The Spaniard who had come of age since 1900 would also anticipate violence from the anarchists. In 1897, 1912 and 1919 individual anarchists had assassinated the prime ministers in the naïve terrorist belief that by getting rid of the man at the top they would strike an effective blow at social injustice. Anarchists were partially responsible for the violence of the Tragic Week in Barcelona, and for numerous killings of strike-breakers, bosses and policemen in connection with the great wave of industrial strikes between 1917 and 1923. Forced underground by the Primo de Rivera dictatorship, a militant minority had organized the Federación Anarquista Ibérica (FAI) in 1927. Although the great majority of anarchists never themselves resorted to violence, they admitted, tolerated or feared their militant minority. In the years 1931–33 they accepted FAI leadership in a series of strikes intended to overthrow the new Republic.

Republicanism and anticlericalism were central features of Spanish political life in the early 1930s. *Above:* the pedestal of a monarchist monument decorated with Republican posters during the April 1931 elections. *Below:* a Carmelite convent set alight by hostile demonstrators.

— Dóna'm els "calés", segueix-me i calla.

Left: Give me the 'swag' and follow me in silence. Rightist cartoon from *Mirador* attacking the minority Spanish Anarchist Federation (FAI), a militant anarchist group which took the lead in the strikes organized by the National Confederation of Labor (CNT) in the first years of the Republic.

Below: popular woodcuts of 1920 illustrating famous anarchist books: *The Conquest of Bread, God and the State, The Individual and Society* and *The Banquet of Life.*

LIBROS ANARQUISTAS FAMOSOS

LA CONQUISTA DEL PAN

DIOS Y EL ESTADO

EL INDIVIDUO Y LA SOCIEDAD

EL BANQUETE DE LA VIDA

Several of the Republic's prominent personalities. From left to right, Mayor Rico of Madrid, Largo Caballero, Minister of Labor, Miguel de Unamuno, Rector of the University of Salamanca, and Indalecio Prieto, Minister of Works.

Alcalá-Zamora proclaims the Republic from the balcony of the Ministry of the Interior in Madrid, 14 April 1931.

Catalan peasants parade in Barcelona in support of the Republic on the second anniversary of its foundation.

Nevertheless, during the first three years of its existence the Republic of 1931 appeared to be setting a new and hopeful course for Spain. It provided immediate relief to thousands of semi-starving rural laborers and substantially raised wages for farm labor. It rapidly expanded the dam- and canal-building program which had been inaugurated by Primo de Rivera for purposes of flood control and agricultural irrigation. It built primary schools and expanded university facilities. It separated Church and state, and made legal divorce possible for the first time in Spanish history. It undertook an army reform intended both to improve the technical quality of the military and to reduce through voluntary retirements the oversize officer corps. It granted regional autonomy in internal administration, education and culture to the province of Catalonia, which in recent decades had become increasingly conscious of its own cultural identity and had been particularly restive under the dictatorship.

President Alcalá-Zamora and his wife vote in the 1933 election, the first regular Cortes election in which women were entitled to participate.

Poster issued by the National Institute for the Social Insurance of Motherhood. The slogan reads: 'The future belongs to the people who nurture the sources of life.'

The Republic was also committed to complete political liberty. Its elections were the most honest in Spanish history. Its press, and its spectrum of political parties, was the most varied in Spanish experience. But the Spanish Republic, like the French Third Republic in its early years, was not the enthusiastic choice of most Spaniards; it was simply the régime which divided them least. Career military officers, high civil servants and judges were apt to be monarchist at heart even if they felt no love for the exiled King. The Church hierarchy never reconciled itself to the creation of a laic republic. The largest conservative bloc, the Catholic Confederation of Autonomous Right Parties, led by Gil Robles, refused to declare its loyalty to the new Republic as such. It adopted an 'accidentalist' position, arguing that Catholic interests were permanent and that forms of government were transitory. The largest left-wing party, the Socialists, took part in the coalition government of the Republican leader Manuel Azaña from 1931 to 1933. But at all times their leaders doubted the wisdom of cabinet participation, and after losing the elections of 1933 the majority of Socialists, especially the younger worker, student and peasant members, thought of the Republic only as a transitional régime on the road to a fully Socialist society.

Had the world of the 1930s been a stable and peaceful world, and had there been time for Republican social reforms to take root, the Spanish Republic of 1931, like the French Third Republic, might in the course of a few decades have stabilized itself and become identified with a wide spectrum of national interests. But two very important factors deprived the Spanish Republic of any such opportunity. One was the acute problem of the landless peasantry in Spain itself; the other was the rise of Fascism in Europe.

Ever since the turn of the century the Spanish government had publicly acknowledged the need for land reform. In northern Spain, generally speaking, peasants could make a tolerable living from land which they either owned or held on secure leases, and their surplus numbers could emigrate freely to Latin America or move to the developing industrial centers. In southern Spain, however, between two and three million landless peasants depended upon seasonal labor, at very low wages. Psychologically they were maimed by a sometimes suave, sometimes brutal, master-servant relationship with the powerful landlords; and they were carefully controlled by the rural police, the famous Civil Guard. They took part in occasional desperate strikes, and they dreamed of a millennial revolution which would somehow create a just, voluntary, collectivist society. They did not have the means or the initiative to emigrate in substantial numbers, but thousands of them entered the factories of Catalonia where they swelled the ranks of the anarcho-syndicalist labor federation, the Confederación Nacional de Trabajo (CNT).

The Spanish government began, as early as 1902, to make a thorough study of rural landownership, and practically every prominent political personality between 1902 and 1931 made statements about the need for land reform. But no specific steps were taken actually to redistribute land. In September 1932 the Constituent Cortes of the Republic passed an agrarian reform law, but one which was completely inadequate for at least three separate reasons. The Republican–Socialist majority could not decide whether it preferred individual or collective ownership of whatever land was to be transferred to the peasants. It also could not decide on the type of financial compensation to be given to the expropriated owners, and it simply did not have the financial means to pay prices

The agrarian reform law – intended to benefit poor areas like this village in Extremadura – was one of the Republic's most publicized and least effective social measures.

Civil Guards and peasants,
Castilblanco, 1932.

per hectare that would have come remotely close to the market value of the land. The philosophical conflicts, the timidities and doubts and the financial inadequacy were all disguised beneath a labyrinth of legal complications such that even the approximately 10,000 families who acquired temporary title to some 200,000 hectares in the period 1932–35 would have had to wait nine years to acquire full title!

The Spanish countryside witnessed naked social conflict throughout the Republican era. In the spring of 1931 the new government, at the urging of the Socialist Minister of Labor, Francisco Largo Caballero, passed a Law of Municipal Boundaries which was intended to protect the local employment rights of rural workers by guaranteeing that all laborers resident in a given town would work in the harvest before any outsiders were hired. But the disadvantages turned out to be greater than the advantages. Thousands of landless farm workers depended on moving freely from province to province as different crops ripened. The law interfered both with the efficiency of the total harvest and with the normal economic pattern for the harvest workers. On 31 December 1931 peasants in the Extremaduran village of Castilblanco first murdered and then desecrated the bodies of four Civil Guards whom they accused of having mistreated unemployed peasant strikers. On 5 January 1932 nervous Civil Guards in the town of Arnedo fired into a crowd of marching

workers, killing six and wounding sixteen. In October 1932 landlords in Salamanca and Extremadura withheld large quantities of
land from cultivation in order to 'discipline' their 'rebellious'
peasants and also drive up the price of wheat. In 1933 numerous
farms were burned in Andalusia and a handful of landlords was
lynched. Although rural wages had been greatly increased in the
years 1931–33, sometimes as much as doubled, there was a notice-
able increase in the number of rural strikes during 1933.

In December 1933 the anarchists in Catalonia attempted a 'revolutionary' strike which was intended to collectivize both land and a
few local factories. In March 1934 they called a general strike in
Saragossa for the purpose of freeing the political prisoners taken in
December, and this well-organized strike tied up the city for almost
six weeks. Then in May, the peasants of Extremadura, many of
whom had recently joined Socialist-sponsored unions, threatened to
strike in the forthcoming June harvest. The government of Alejandro Lerroux sponsored arbitration agreements which made substantial wage concessions and on 5 June, the day scheduled for the
strike, less than 20 per cent of the rural workers in a handful of villages
actually went out. But the Minister of the Interior, claiming that the
time had come to crush the 'Marxist Revolution,' arrested four
Socialist deputies and several thousand peasants. Hundreds of the
latter were transported by freight car to jails in distant Castilian

Civil Guards advance on a
crowd of demonstrators:
Ramón Casas, *The Attack*.

towns. At almost the same time, on 8 June 1934, the Spanish Supreme Court ruled unconstitutional a moderate agrarian reform law passed by the Catalan regional government on behalf of the small vinegrowers of that province. The technical legal issues were arguable either way, but the decision came down firmly on the side of central government and landlord power against regional autonomy and peasant needs. Wherever one's political sympathies lay, there was no missing the critical nature of rural problems by the summer of 1934. Government-sponsored land reform had proved to be totally inadequate. Clashes between peasants and police were on the increase. Landlords were curbing acreage, and some were fleeing to the cities in fear of rural violence. Medium-sized farms were also being sold at a loss by owners who could not simultaneously pay the increased wages and cope with inefficiency, political turmoil and occasional sabotage. At the same time both the anarchists and the Socialists were organizing the peasants and promising them a collectivized society which could not possibly be achieved without a revolution.

The second grave problem preventing the stabilization of the Republic in 1934 was the aggressive nature of European Fascism. The founder of Fascism, Benito Mussolini, had been in power in Italy since 1922, but in its initial decade his régime, though brutal and swaggering, did not directly threaten European stability. The Primo dictatorship in Spain had in some ways been modeled on Mussolini's, but it had been distinctly milder in both action and doctrine. The entire picture changed with the rise of Hitler in Germany. From 1930 on it was very evident from the nature of Hitler's speeches and from the activities of his storm troops that if he once achieved power he would destroy all political and intellectual liberty within Germany and prepare for a war of revenge against the powers which had defeated Germany in the First World War. In January 1933 he was appointed Chancellor by the aged and perhaps senile President Hindenburg. In March the Catholic Center Party abandoned its parliamentary tradition by joining in the vote which gave Hitler the emergency powers he needed to establish his dictatorship. In July 1933 the Vatican signed a Concordat with the Nazi régime, and the Center Party, already demoralized, was officially dissolved. In February 1934 the right-wing Chancellor of the Austrian Republic, Engelbert Dollfuss, closed parliament and put down in blood the subsequent protest strikes of the Socialist workers of Vienna.

In the Cortes elections of November 1933 the Catholic confederation of Gil Robles, known by its acronym as the CEDA, emerged as the strongest single party in the chamber. Because of Gil Robles' 'accidentalist' position concerning forms of government, the conservative Catholic President of the Republic, Niceto Alcalá-Zamora, refused in early 1934 even to permit CEDA ministers to be appointed to the cabinet. But by the fall of 1934 the parliamentary situation was becoming impossible. On the one hand liberal Republicans and

Estate-owners from Catalonia arrive in Madrid to protest at the land reform measures passed by the Generalitat, the autonomous Catalan parliament.

Socialists, as well as the anarchists, were in the opposition. On the other hand the President dared not give power to the CEDA, which was organizing Fascist-type youth groups and increasingly employing the Fascist vocabulary. Successive governments headed by Alejandro Lerroux and Ricardo Samper temporized without successfully appeasing either the Right or the Left. In the streets Socialist and anarchist students, newsboys and militant workers engaged in urban guerrilla fighting against monarchist and Fascist students and newsboys.

When the Cortes reconvened from the summer recess on 1 October, the CEDA demanded that Gil Robles be named Prime Minister. The President remained adamant on this point, but felt that he could not indefinitely exclude from the cabinet the largest single party represented in the Cortes. He tried to compromise by once more naming Lerroux Prime Minister while specifying that the CEDA was to hold several ministries. The entire Left reacted immediately. A group of moderate and Left-Republican leaders, united by their loyalty to the Republican régime and their fear of Gil Robles, told the President that if he allowed the CEDA to enter the government they would break off all relations with 'existing institutions.' The Socialist Party, chanting the slogan 'Better Vienna than Berlin,' voted to call a general strike throughout the country.

In the complex series of events which followed these proclamations, three main strands are essential to an understanding of the Spanish Civil War: the general strike, the regional revolt in Catalonia and the revolutionary commune in the Asturias. The nationwide general strike of 5 October was almost a total failure. In none of the industrial cities did large numbers participate, and in the countryside the peasants were still demoralized from the failure of their own strike in June. The anarchists on the whole abstained, and the Socialists themselves were very divided. Largo Caballero had been trying for months to create a working alliance between the left wing of the Socialists and the several small Marxist parties in Aragon and Catalonia. But these efforts had by no means overcome either regional suspicion of the Madrid-centered Socialist Party or the ideological differences with Trotskyites and former anarchists. Had the general strike of 5 October been the only reaction to the parliamentary crisis it would simply have illustrated the disunity and the sheer inefficacy of working-class leadership.

In Catalonia the reaction took the form of a regional rising against the central government. Nationalist feeling had been increasing for some months owing to the fact that the Catalan public interpreted delays in the transfer of various powers to their local government as anti-Catalan sabotage on the part of Madrid. To the normal suspicion of Castilian motives was added the fact that the elections of late 1933 had produced a conservative victory nationally and a left victory in Catalonia. The small farmers were particularly bitter over the Supreme Court decision declaring unconstitutional the Catalan land reform. At the same time the Catalan government, under President Luis Companys, was threatened on its right by the rise of a local Fascist movement, the green-shirted Estat Català. Now on 5 October the Madrid government had declared the *estado de guerra*, a national emergency, to deal with the general strike. Pressured by rising nationalism and a developing Fascist party at home, and reacting to what seemed to portend a Fascist government in Madrid, Companys on the evening of 6 October proclaimed 'the Catalan state within the federal Spanish Republic.' Owing to the patience and common sense of General Domingo Batet, the commanding general of the army division stationed in Barcelona, the Catalan rising was suppressed with a minimum of bloodshed and the Companys government was arrested peaceably on the morning of 7 October.

The truly grave events occurred in the northern mining province of Asturias. Here, during the spring and summer of 1934, Socialists, Communists, anarchists and even Trotskyites had managed to achieve minimal agreements on the need for unity against the threat of Fascism. Part of the Socialist leadership, notably Indalecio Prieto, had helped to smuggle small but symbolically important quantities of arms to the miners. Asturias had been the starting-point of the long Christian Reconquest of Spain in the Middle Ages. Its ardent revolutionaries in 1934 were determined that it should witness the birth of the Socialist millennium. On 5 October revolutionary miners attacked several Civil Guard and police barracks, and collected all the weapons they could lay hands on. Intoning the slogan 'Unión, Hermanos Proletarios' (Union, Proletarian Brothers), they marched, about 8,000 strong, on the provincial capital, Oviedo. In that city of 80,000 inhabitants, and in the villages they had occupied on their march, they attempted to establish a commune, expropriating large businesses and factories, rationing food and medical services, trying ardently to win over the frightened population, and lynching about forty Civil Guards, property owners and priests. The government, fearing that conscript soldiers might not fire on the revolutionary miners, and acting on the advice of Generals Francisco Franco and Manuel Goded, used contingents of Moorish troops and of the Foreign Legion to suppress the commune. Landing in Gijón and Avilés on 8 October, they had reoccupied the city of Oviedo by the 12th, and by 18 October they had secured the surrender of the last mining villages. According to the probably incomplete figures given by the Ministry of the Interior early in 1935, about 1,300 were killed and 3,000 wounded during the actual fighting.

During the first three weeks of October, while these multiple events were occurring, the Spanish public could not know in detail what was transpiring in widely separated parts of the peninsula. But certain things were very clear, and very frightening. The President and the Cortes had been unable to maintain parliamentary government. An attempted general strike had led to the declaration of a national emergency, with consequent censorship and police rule. Two armed uprisings had occurred, one in the name of Catalan regional liberty and one in the name of proletarian revolution. The specter of revolutionary violence, and the counter-use of Moorish troops, had horrified Spaniards of all persuasions. These things had taken place against a background of heavy-handed police action against strikers, rising peasant agitation, rising Catalan nationalism, the radicalization of a large proportion of the Socialists and the strident advances of German and Austrian Fascism. Luckily the general strike and the Catalan rising had been contained with a minimum of violence. But the Asturian rising had challenged the entire basis of the parliamentary Republic, and the government had suppressed it with troops whom the great majority of Spaniards considered to be both foreigners and savages.

Indalecio Prieto, ablest of the parliamentary Socialists and co-leader, with Azaña, of the Republican-Socialist alliance of 1931–33.

Rising violence on both Left and Right threatened the basis of the young Republic. In this incident in 1933 the Madrid–Bilbao express was derailed by a bomb placed on the track.

Salvador Dali, *A Premonition of the Civil War* (1936).

Chapter Two

FROM THE OCTOBER REVOLT TO THE MILITARY RISING OF JULY 1936

In their total impact the events of October 1934 came close to destroying the three-year-old Republic. For many weeks the Lerroux government had little control over the Asturian repression. Each of the triumphant military units (Civil Guards, Assault Guards and Foreign Legion) shot batches of prisoners without any sort of accountability. Memoirs of survivors and later Cortes investigations suggest that the total so executed may well have been greater than the approximately 1,300 killed in actual fighting. A soldier of the Foreign Legion assassinated a well-known journalist in the streets of Oviedo. Civil Guard Major Doval employed sadistic sexual tortures ostensibly in order to find out where the miners had hidden their remaining arms after the 18 October surrender. Courts-martial of civilian leaders handed down death sentences, sometimes for persons who had demonstrably opposed the armed rising. Neither the Prime Minister nor the President desired a brutal repression. Major Doval was removed after public exposure of his methods, and all but two of the death sentences were commuted, much to the chagrin of the CEDA chieftain Gil Robles and the monarchist deputies in the Cortes. The uncensored right-wing press was filled with what later turned out to be utterly unfounded tales of miners raping nuns and gouging out the eyes of children. The censored left-wing press, getting its stories largely from French newspapers, was able occasionally to counter with exaggerated tales of Moorish rape and generally accurate tales of police and military brutality.

The fact that the Asturian miners had, in the name of anti-Fascism, resorted to arms gave the government an apparent opportunity to discredit the entire Left. Dozens of Catalan and Basque municipal governments, and the Catalan parliament, were suspended on the grounds that their political conflicts with Madrid amounted to a direct attack on the sovereignty of the Spanish state. In the rest of the country municipal government and rural wage arbitration juries with Socialist majorities were suspended on the grounds that their

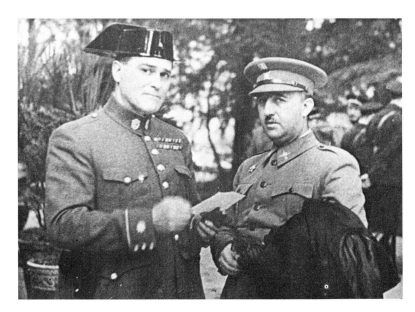

Above: Major Doval, a prominent leader of the Asturian repression, with General Franco, his Minister of War. *Below:* Yves Allix, *The Surrender* (1933), a brutal portrayal of the savagery that pervaded Spain in the 1930s.

Opposite: a demonstration in Barcelona in support of the Asturian miners, and, *below,* street fighting in Madrid.

Manuel Azaña, Republican leader.

Gil Robles, leader of the Catholic Conservative Federation (CEDA).

Socialist affiliation made them co-responsible for the armed rising in Asturias. Altogether some 30,000 to 40,000 political prisoners spent the year 1935 in jail awaiting trial on vague conspiracy charges. Most of them were not physically mistreated, but the experience radicalized their politics. Students, small-town Socialist officials and militant workers cemented new friendships and developed broader class sympathies while reading and discussing the works of Marx, Bakunin, Tolstoy, Nietzsche, Lenin and Stalin. Largo Caballero, who had been moving left since 1933 and who now read Marx for the first time, became the hero of young fellow-prisoners who regretted their own bourgeois background and who idolized him as an authentic proletarian leader.

In June 1935 the seven members of the Companys government received thirty-year sentences for their part in the Barcelona events of 6 October. Largo Caballero was acquitted when it became obvious that he had neither supplied arms to anyone nor taken part in the minor street fighting in Madrid. Meanwhile the monarchists, in Cortes debate, attempted to lay the moral responsibility for the entire October revolt at the door of the principal Left-Republican leader and former Prime Minister, Manuel Azaña. In the subsequent balloting the Carlists, the Alphonsine monarchists and the CEDA voted against Azaña. The conservative Republicans, the Basque Nationalists, the Catalan Left and the entire Socialist bloc voted for him. The line-up was to be the same in July 1936.

While the government month by month extended the *estado de alarma* and the press censorship, political emotions and ideologies hardened on both the Right and the Left. Socialist youth turned increasingly from the reformist to the revolutionary position. The democratic Republic, fearful of any fundamental social change, was merely a wayside station on the road to a collectivized society. The Asturian revolt had been a heroic defeat, also an exemplary one in that the workers had shown that unity among Socialists, Communists and anarchists was possible. The young Socialists, looking to Largo Caballero for leadership, hoped to win over the naïve and confused anarchist masses and to create a society which would be egalitarian and largely voluntary, and which would imitate the earlier phases of the Russian Revolution, before power had passed from the local worker and peasant Soviets to the centralized party bureaucracy and police.

Several small, Fascist-type organizations competed increasingly with the Socialists and anarchists for the attention of students, workers and peasants. Rejecting the class orientation, the atheism and the internationalism of the leftist ideologies, they called for a 'national' revolution on behalf of all 'producers.' They recognized the justice of Marxist social criticism, were violently anti-capitalist in their rhetoric, and spoke of nationalizing banks and public services, also of distributing land in the form of individual family farms. They interpreted the Asturian revolt as the result of international Marxist,

Masonic and sometimes Jewish plotting. Young Catholics also turned away from gradualist, parliamentary government. The youth organization sponsored by Gil Robles's CEDA, and the monarchist youth groups, were equally vehement in their anti-Marxist and nationalist orientation, but were not anti-capitalist and concerned themselves principally with the maintenance of a 'traditional,' hierarchical and officially Catholic Spain. What all these groups – Socialist, anarchist, Fascist and Catholic – had in common was their disgust with the parliamentary Republic, their combative ardor, their press and leaflet propaganda, and their assumption that a fundamental test of force was coming between the Right and the Left.

In the midst of this political effervescence the President and the Prime Minister decided, in December 1935, to hold new parliamentary elections. There were three coalition lists. The government itself, based upon numerically very small middle-of-the-road Republican parties, hoped that the voters would flock to the moderate centrist banner. They reasoned that the commutation of death sentences and the restoration of civilian authority should appeal to the moderate Left, and that the maintenace of public order and the deference shown to military and Church leaders should reassure the moderate Right. Finally they hoped that, in the face of rising militancy on both the Left and the Right, the majority of Spaniards would vote for the Center.

The coalition of Catholics and monarchists confidently expected a victory which would give full power to Gil Robles, power which he

The 1936 election. Billboard displaying posters for the Left coalition, and, on their right, a Popular Front placard appealing for amnesty for political prisoners.

31

would surely use to reverse those legislative acts which had reduced, however slightly, the pre-1931 prerogatives of the army, the Church, the landlords and industrial employers. Nothing was offered in the way of a positive program, nor any ideas concerning the future form of the Spanish state. The Popular Front coalition of Left-Republicans, Socialists and Communists promised amnesty for all political prisoners and a return to the reformist program of 1931, with two significant changes: the Socialists would support, but not actually participate in, the new Azaña government, and land reform would be greatly speeded up.

The style of the six-week campaign was greatly influenced by contemporary European models. The chanted slogan, 'All power to the Chief,' the enormous photographs of Gil Robles and the deliberate programmatic vagueness plainly imitated the style of Mussolini. As in Italy and Austria, the coalition of the Right represented an uneasy working alliance of Catholics, Fascists and monarchists. The Popular Front agreement clearly reflected the changed orientation of the Communist International at its 1935 World Congress. Instead of being stigmatized as 'social fascists,' as in pre-Hitler days, the Socialists and all 'progressive' middle-class elements were to be welcomed in a broad anti-Fascist, non-revolutionary alliance. But also, since the governing program of the coalition was purely 'bourgeois' in content, Communists and Socialists should support the government but not accept cabinet assignments.

On Sunday, 16 February, the atmosphere was calmer than most people had anticipated, and the voter turnout was the largest in Spanish history. The Popular Front gained 257 out of a total of 473 deputies, 20 more than an absolute majority. The Center obtained only about 450,000 votes. The victorious Left received 4,700,000 and the Right some 4,000,000. Despite the impassioned campaign oratory the relative voting strength of the predominantly Catholic Right and the predominantly Socialist Left had changed very little in two years. The Right had increased its total by about 600,000, most of whom had voted for Lerroux in 1933. The Left had increased its absolute total by about 700,000, most of whom were anarchists who had abstained in 1933.

Although the election had taken place peaceably, it was followed by months of frenzied agitation, complete uncertainty as to the future and considerable disorder in many parts of the country. The Left organized an unending series of victory parades in the major cities, featuring both revolutionary Marxist and anarchist slogans. Many speeches and editorials intimated that the life of the Republican government would be brief and that the proletariat must prepare to advance towards Socialism. The attitude was symbolized by comparing Azaña's role with that of Kerensky and Largo Caballero's with that of Lenin in the Russian Revolution of 1917. In April the Cortes voted, 238 to 5, to oust President Alcalá-Zamora. This impeachment indicated the dangerous polarization occurring throughout the body

Huge May Day celebrations in 1936 (*opposite*, part of the parade in Madrid) demonstrating solidarity with Soviet Russia and with leftist movements throughout Europe contributed to bourgeois and aristocratic fears of Socialist revolution.

politic. The Left held the President guilty of having authorized the use of Moorish troops in the Asturias, and they were convinced that if he remained in office he would block all significant social legislation. The Right abstained from defending him because he had refused power to Gil Robles in October 1934 and because he had favored leniency in the aftermath of the October rising. The entire Popular Front, supported by a number of conservative Republicans, then promoted Prime Minister Azaña to the Presidency, but the revolutionary wing of the Socialist Party refused to allow the most able of the parliamentary Socialists, Indalecio Prieto, to become Prime Minister. From 8 May until the outbreak of the Civil War Spain was 'governed' by a minority cabinet of Left-Republicans headed by the intellectually mediocre and physically tubercular Santiago Casares Quiroga.

During the spring of 1936 the peasants in western and southern Spain conducted their own land reform. The Popular Front had promised speedier land distribution, the fields lay uncultivated and the plowing season had arrived. Motivated by a combination of sheer hunger and messianic hope, and migrating with oxcarts, cloth bundles and a miscellany of furnishings and tools, they exercised squatters' rights. If the Civil Guard tried to move them off, they usually avoided a direct clash and simply returned a day or two later. Most of the landlords felt it safer to remain in Madrid or Seville until circumstances would be more favorable to the assertion of property rights. Numerous brief strikes, most of them economic but some of them political or simply euphoric in motivation, took place in the cities. On 1 June some 70,000 building workers downed tools in Madrid. The strike was intended to cement cooperation between the UGT (the Socialist Unión General de Trabajadores) and the CNT, but when the main economic demands had been met and when it became evident that the continuation of the strike would be likely to bring down the Casares government, the Socialists voted to accept the available agreement with the employers, while the anarchists wished to continue. Meanwhile, in Malaga, UGT and CNT gunmen shot down several rival leaders, and the civil governor on 15 June closed the headquarters of both labor federations. Catalonia and the Basque country, on the other hand, remained quiet throughout the spring.

The reaction of the Right following the election was equally varied and confused. For the first forty-eight hours the air was thick with rumors of a military *coup* whose purpose would be to annul the Left's electoral victory. But the defeated CEDA leaders freely acknowledged the electoral results, and affirmed their belief in parliamentary methods. Later in the spring some of them applauded the Azaña legislative program while warning that strikes, disorders and revolutionary propaganda were causing their own followers to turn increasingly to the anti-parliamentary and pro-Fascist Falange. Gil Robles attacked the government for failure to maintain order and to protect the Church against sporadic violence. The monarchist leader, and former Minister of Finance under Primo de Rivera, José Calvo Sotelo, also stressed the public order problem, but claimed in addition that a Marxist revolution was already occurring and that the government, in its hatred of the military, was making generals out of corporals. Calvo Sotelo, who sonorously referred to the army as the 'dorsal column of the nation,' was privately sounding out conservative deputies as to their attitude towards a possible military *coup*.

Meanwhile the Azaña cabinet attempted to fulfil the pledges of the Popular Front pact. Immediate amnesty was granted to all the political prisoners jailed after the October revolt. In the confusion not a few common criminals were released too. The suspended municipal governments were restored to office, and the regional Catalan government of Luis Companys returned in triumph to Barcelona. Rural rent payments were suspended in Extremadura and Andalusia, preparatory to the resumption of land reform. When the peasants began squatting on vacant lands in March the government, in the person of the Minister of Agriculture, ratified the land occupations and tried to help out with seed, tools, transportation and credit. About 500,000 hectares were occupied in March and April (the spring plowing season) and another 150,000 by 18 July. Some 80,000 to 100,000 peasant families thus received land (as against a total of about 10,000 legally incomplete transfers in the years 1932–35).

Azaña was well aware that no matter what positive reforms were accomplished, the government must show its ability to maintain public order. Early in March he demanded that Largo Caballero use his influence to end the monotonous but worrisome victory parades. As a warning to both Fascists and anarchists he extended the *estado de alarma*. Hoping both to deflate the revolutionaries and to reassure the middle class, he retained newspaper censorship of stories describing disorders. In agreement with the rightist leaders he postponed the municipal elections scheduled for April, both sides acknowledging that they could not be conducted fairly in the reigning atmosphere of intimidation. Tacit cooperation between the Church and the government resulted in quiet, orderly processions during Holy Week, and the Vatican, which had refused to receive a Republican ambassador in 1931, gave its *placet* to the naming of Luis Zulueta in 1936. Church schools also remained open until 20 May, at which date the government, acting on reports of threatened arson, closed them. Final examinations were interrupted by the order. Catholic parents flooded the government with protest letters, and the action admitted, in effect, to a rising tide of anticlerical agitation which the government was not certain it could contain.

In the spring of 1936, and indeed ever since the October 1934 events, the Spanish people as a whole was passionately involved in politics; but it was extremely difficult to gauge the force of public opinion. In the February elections the voters had been presented with

An Andalusian peasant desecrates a Madonna, evidence of the strength of the anticlerical feeling during the spring of 1936.

coalition lists rather than separate parties. But they could, if they wished, express preferences for individuals within a list. Rightist voters gave their preference to men of the CEDA, not to monarchists or military officers. Leftist voters indicated their preference for the moderate Socialists Julián Besteiro and Luís Jiménez de Asúa over Largo Caballero and other candidates of the party's left wing. In February the Falange numbered only about 10,000, and elected no deputy. The Communist Party also numbered about 10,000, and their general secretary, José Díaz, was elected on the Popular Front list, but with still fewer votes than the Left-Socialists. The elections, then, seemed to indicate a desire for firm, but moderate, civilian government, either that of Azaña or of Gil Robles.

But while a majority of voters may have hoped for such an outcome, the new government was unable to mobilize that moderate opinion. The militant leaders and activist youth on both the Right and the Left behaved as if, in their opinion, the election had settled nothing. What Left-Socialists, Communists and anarchists meant by 'supporting' the Republican government was that they would insist on the rapid fulfilment of the electoral program and then push on to a fully Socialist or collectivized society, albeit with vague and contradictory ideas about how and when that desired revolution would occur. On the Right the monarchists, Fascists and activist military assumed that the revolutionary rhetoric would soon be put into practice, and that neither a moderately Left Azaña government nor a moderately Right Gil Robles government would be capable of protecting property and religion.

In these circumstances the Socialist and Communist youth organizations fused under Left-Socialist and Communist leadership, and the youth who had followed Gil Robles for four years streamed into the rapidly growing Falange. Both groups spent evenings and Sundays ostentatiously engaging in para-military training under the guidance of politically active army officers or Assault Guards. Rival parades and political rallies challenged each other with taunts, fists, clubs and occasional shots. Anonymous newspaper vendors and well-known political personalities were the objects of numerous attempted assassinations, and when some of these resulted in death there could be both verbal and physical violence at the funeral ceremonies. Owing to both censorship and panic, we will never know even approximately how many persons actually died in the street violence between 17 February and 18 July. Several dozen shootings and bombing were reported in detail by the press, enough to give the public the jitters and to discredit the Azaña and Casares governments for failure to maintain public order. In the Cortes on 16 June Gil Robles claimed that 269 people had died in street fighting or by assassination since 17 February, but the figures are impossible to verify.

Well-known personalities from outside the Popular Front, such as the world-famous Dr Gregorio Marañón, the regional CEDA leaders Giménez Fernández and Luis Lucía, and the conservative

Republican Miguel Maura, attempted to bolster the government by crediting its probity and its efforts to achieve a measure of social justice, and by defending it against panic reports of complete anarchy. The moderate Socialist Indalecio Prieto was unambiguous in his warnings that continued strikes and disorders would bring not Socialism but military dictatorship. Shots were fired at him as he came on to the speaker's platform in an Andalusian village, and he received several written death threats. In May and June he was accompanied by a bodyguard of Asturian veterans, and sometimes by Dr Juan Negrín, a personal friend and the future wartime Prime Minister of the Republic.

In the divided Socialist Party those who had witnessed the sufferings of the Asturian miners supported Prieto, those whose direct experience was only rhetorical supported Largo Caballero. Moreover, during the weeks preceding the outbreak of the Civil War, the militant Socialists were having second thoughts. In the Madrid building trades strike the UGT leaders were ready for a moderate settlement and were anxious not to embarrass the Casares government by worker intransigence. In the 30 June elections for party

Rally of young Falangists in Burgos, 1936, watched by a group of nuns from a balcony, top left.

Generals Franco and Emilio Mola, principal chieftains of the military *coup* against the Republican government.

offices the Prieto faction gained ground. On the other hand, the party was so deeply split, on personal as well as political grounds, between its two main leaders that the party conference originally scheduled for late June was postponed until October. Official Franquist historians have written that Largo Caballero intended to establish a Soviet Spain, that the revolution was to occur between 11 May and 29 June, and that the date was then postponed until 1 August. Actually, in late June and the first days of July Largo was in France and England, conferring with very respectable trade union leaders. But his revolutionary rhetoric gave a wonderful propaganda excuse to men who were indeed planning to seize state power.

From the moment of the Popular Front's electoral victory, the activist military began planning to overthrow the resulting government. The outgoing Prime Minister, Portela Valladares, claimed that on 17 February the army Chief of Staff, General Francisco Franco, offered his services to annul the elections. Several CEDA leaders and high army officers have said that civilian rightists urged Franco and other generals to launch a *coup*, but that Franco refused. Generals Sebastián Pozas of the Civil Guard and Núñez del Prado of the air force warned Portela of widespread nervousness in the barracks, and in the cafés reactionary officers spoke openly of using the army to prevent an 'anti-national' revolution. The newly installed Azaña government took the precaution of removing from Madrid the high officers who would be the obvious candidates to lead a military rising. On 21 February General Franco was assigned to the Canary Islands and the widely respected monarchist General Manuel Goded to Barcelona.

Serious planning for a *pronunciamiento* began in late February, and the initiative was taken by monarchist generals and colonels working with the membership of the officers' organization, the Unión Militar Española (UME). It was quickly agreed that General Sanjurjo, living in Portugal since the failure of his August 1932 revolt, should again lead the rising. But it was necessary to have strong organizational planning within Spain, and it was necessary to involve high ranking officers who were not monarchists. Colonel Valentín Galarza, acting for Sanjurjo, met with a number of generals early in March, among them Franco and Emilio Mola. Franco refused to commit himself on this occasion. Mola had been the last Director-General of Security under the King, and as such had advised Alfonso in April 1931 that the army would not fight to maintain his throne. He was therefore not beloved of the monarchists, but he had a reputation for keen intelligence and relative liberalism. The Republican government distrusted him less than it did most generals, and within the army he would be able to work as a 'professional' military man with both Republican and monarchist colleagues, thus avoiding a polarization of the officer corps. After the March meeting Mola emerged as the principal planner.

Most commentators on the Civil War have stated that the Republican government in the spring of 1936 was incomprehensibly blind to the danger of a military uprising. Such a judgment is not correct. Azaña began by removing Generals Goded and Franco from Madrid. While assignment to the island provinces permitted them to transact their affairs far from government eyes, it also removed them from the center of the communications network and from direct contact with their like-minded colleagues. However conscious the government might be of the hostile feelings of leading officers, it had no sure evidence that could have justified cashiering them. When it appeared that a rising was planned for 25 April the government rapidly transferred its potential leaders, reassigning Colonel Orgaz to the Canaries and Colonel Varela to Cádiz. Those generals chosen for key staff and command posts in Madrid – Masquelet, Miaja, Núñez del Prado, Hernández Sarabia – turned out on 18 July to be loyal to the government.

Various other shifts of personnel in the course of the spring interfered with the military plotting by upsetting potential chains of command and by locating loyal officers in important garrisons. The assignment of General Gómez Morato to Melilla made it necessary to depend there upon lower-ranking officers. Generals Molero and Batet, assigned respectively to Valladolid and Burgos, asked embarrassing questions of their colleague, Mola, and had to be seized by the plotters on 18 July. In Catalonia the Companys government saw to it that the commanding officers assigned to Civil and Assault Guard units were loyal. This had the adverse effect of increasing the influence of reactionaries in the barracks, but it meant that in a crisis the regular 'forces of order' could be depended upon by the Generalitat.

It is nevertheless true that in June and early July Prime Minister Casares, and perhaps also President Azaña, were mistakenly discounting the frequent and specific warnings which they received. It is quite possible that, having survived the first great scare period just after the elections, and having reassigned the potential leaders, they underestimated the danger in June. It is equally possible that, because of the continuing strikes and the mounting disorder in the streets, they were far more anxious about infantile leftists and about Falangist and Carlist youth than about the professional military as *immediate* sources of trouble. The personal situation of the Prime Minister probably also played a role. Casares attended cabinet meetings and Cortes sessions running a fever caused by chronic tuberculosis. The most insistent warnings came from Prieto – the Socialist who would have been Prime Minister if his party had given its consent. It must have been a desperate personal affirmation for Casares to deny the evidence tendered by an overshadowing colleague concerning a crisis he would have been literally too ill to face.

The government did make one truly fatal error: the assignment of General Mola to Pamplona. Mola had been commanding the Moroccan army. He was disliked by the monarchists, and the government perhaps thought that he would be safely isolated from political intrigue if assigned the relatively small garrison in Navarre. Actually the supposedly liberal Mola, who had conceived a violent hatred for Azaña due to the latter's army reforms, was happy to hold the main threads in his hands. Colonel Galarza was his link to the monarchists and to Sanjurjo. Colonel Yagüe of the Foreign Legion was his link to Falangist officers, and to Franco if the latter could be brought into the conspiracy. Raimundo García, editor of the *Diario de Navarra*, and Agustín Lizarza were his able civilian emissaries to the Carlists, a party of ardent Catholic royalists who had fought the constitutional monarchy ever since 1883 on the grounds that it was too secular in spirit. Mola corresponded by courier with the imprisoned young Falangist chief, José Antonio Primo de Rivera. The UME reported to him on sentiment in the barracks, and Santiago Martín Báguenas, chief of police in Madrid, kept him informed of attitudes in the government and the capital.

The planning was by no means easy. The military, including Mola, distrusted their necessary civilian allies. Mola was at times depressed by the evident lack of any large public support for a *pronunciamiento*, and by the fact that a suspicious government kept rotating officers and thus breaking up his potential chains of command. José Antonio made his support conditional on the assurance that the majority of the people would welcome an army régime. The

Carlists insisted on organizing independent units flying their own flag, and only General Sanjurjo, whose father had been a Carlist general, could get them to accept a compromise plan for an all-military directory which would postpone the choice between a monarchy and a corporative state. The rising was first scheduled for 10 July, then for the period 10–20 July. The monarchist chief José Calvo Sotelo had ratified Mola's plans and was hoping to enlist the support of Gil Robles, whom the officers did not trust, but whose support, or at least benevolent neutrality, would be essential to the military directory.

While there is no doubt that a significant fraction of the Spanish army intended to take over the government in July 1936, the Civil War itself was precipitated by the assassination on 12 July of Calvo Sotelo. There had been many political murders and attempted assassinations since February, and Madrid had already been shocked on this Sunday afternoon by the Falangist murder of a popular Assault Guards lieutenant, José Castillo. But no victim of political violence up to this time had been so well known and had held such a key post as Calvo Sotelo. He had been Minister of Finance under Primo de Rivera, and thus possessed greater administrative and executive experience than any other prominent conservative. Speaking candidly for an authoritarian monarchical constitution, and in favor of the army as the guardian of national tradition, he was rapidly replacing Gil Robles as the principal civilian figure on the Right. He was also the political leader most closely in touch with the military plotters. At the same time, both for his personal qualities and for his creation of CAMPSA, the state petroleum monopoly, he was admired by not a few Socialists.

General José Sanjurjo, titular chief of the military rising, killed in an airplane accident on 20 July 1936.

The manner of death was as shocking as the choice of victim. A group of Assault Guards intending to avenge the death of their comrade Lieutenant Castillo knocked at the door of Calvo Sotelo's apartment bearing what looked like a bona-fide warrant for his arrest. A brave man who suspected treachery, and who psychologically was prepared to accept martyrdom, the monarchist chief quietly descended the stairs between these vigilantes. Late the following morning his bullet-ridden body with its marks of violent struggle was identified in the public morgue. The government immediately arrested some fifteen members of Castillo's guard company and vowed that they would receive a speedy, open trial in a civilian court. But the Right was not to be mollified, and whether or not one believed the rightist charges that the Casares government itself was in collusion with the murderers, it was intolerable that a political chieftain of the opposition in a constitutional democratic republic should be slaughtered by uniformed officers driving a government car. The murder of Calvo Sotelo thus precipitated the long-planned military rising, and gave it a moral *élan* it would otherwise have lacked.

Arriba España

JUNTA DE BURGOS
LISBOA

Los Nacionales

MINISTERIO DE PROPAGANDA

Chapter Three

FROM *PRONUNCIAMIENTO* TO INTERNATIONAL CIVIL WAR

Coordinated risings throughout Spanish territory were scheduled to take place on Saturday, 18 July. In Morocco the action was advanced to 5 p.m. on the 17th because loyal troops were about to arrest the plotters in Melilla. Led principally by colonels and majors of the Foreign Legion, the Insurgents seized the main public buildings of Ceuta, Melilla and Tetuán, arrested Generals Gómez Morato and Romerales, detained the civilian High Commissioner Álvarez Buylla, shot the aviators who refused to join them at Tetuán, and on the morning of the 18th broke the general strike called by the labor federations. Meanwhile General Francisco Franco left his post in the Canary Islands in a private English plane which had been arranged for by monarchists. Arriving in Tetuán on 19 July he awarded the first decoration of the Civil War, the Grand Cross of St Ferdinand, to Visir Sidi Ahmed el Ganmia, who had suppressed Moorish demonstrations against the rising.

On the peninsula, events moved swiftly in a number of provinces. In Pamplona General Mola's Carlist troops took to the streets with the cry, 'Viva Cristo Rey' ('Long Live Christ the King'). When the Civil Guard General Rodríguez Medel unaccountably refused to join them he was shot. At Burgos General Dávila arrested his commanding officer, the Republican General Batet, and at Salamanca the Insurgents proclaimed the *estado de guerra* in the town square and shot the few people who protested. In Valladolid Generals Saliquet and Ponte arrested their commanding officer, the former War Minister General Molero. They met sharp resistance from the railroad-workers, but gained full control of the city in about twenty-four hours. In Saragossa General Miguel Cabanellas, a mason and reputed liberal, read the military proclamation in the presence of middle-rank younger officers who made sure that the white-bearded old gentleman played the role expected of him. Madrid sent out his friend and fellow-Republican, General Núñez del Prado, to speak to Cabanellas. Núñez was met at the rail depot by Insurgent officers who

Opposite: The Nationalists. Government propaganda caricaturing the composition of the Nationalist rebellion. On board the *Burgos Junta* (registered at Lisbon) are a German financier, a cardinal, a general and Moorish soldiers.

arrested and later shot him. The CNT and UGT also called a general strike, and scattered resistance continued for several weeks in the working-class districts before all the militants could be disarmed and shot.

Boldest of the first-day victories was that of General Gonzalo Queipo de Llano. On an inspection tour as head of the frontier police, he arrived in Seville late on 17 July. On the 18th he arrested the local commanding officer, General Villa-Abrille, plus the civil governor and the chief of police. With some 200 Insurgent troops he disarmed the local Assault Guards who were thought to be loyal to the government. Then dressing his soldiers in baggy pants and smearing them with walnut juice so that they would look like Moors, he made a series of rapid truck-borne raids on the working-class quarters. On the 19th he told citizens he greatly admired the social accomplishments of the Republic – and would shoot anyone who resisted the military takeover. In the other southern cities of Cádiz, Granada and Córdoba the Insurgents won rapidly, albeit at the cost of a few days' hard street fighting. In strongly Republican Galicia the working-class leaders accepted the officers' protestations of loyalty and agreed on 19 July not to insist on arming the workers. On the 20th, the younger officers arrested Generals Salcedo and Caridad Pita, confused some of their opponents (and perhaps their own troops) by shouting, 'Viva la República,' and in the course of several days broke the sporadic resistance in the cities. In Oviedo the commanding officer, Colonel Aranda, was reputed to be loyal to the Republic.

Arms outstretched in the Fascist salute, supporters acclaim officials of the Insurgent government installed at Burgos.

Graciously providing a train to carry militant workers off to defend threatened Madrid, he then seized the city on behalf of the Insurgents. In these, and in many another factory town, port or mining area, the Insurgents were greatly aided by the refusal of the Casares government to authorize distribution of arms to civilians.

Not all went according to Insurgent plans in these first crucial days. At Badajoz the loyal General Castelló prevented a rising. In Bilbao the municipal government, suspecting the military, intercepted all telephone calls to the barracks, and, with the surprise element lost, no rising occurred. In Jaén and Malaga local officials distributed arms despite Madrid, and armed workers led by Assault Guards defeated the rising. But the critical defeats took place in the two capital cities. In Madrid, where the government had refused to distribute arms on the 18th, a group of young artillery officers and aviators supplied about 5,000 rifles and led working-class detachments which extinguished the rising at the airfields of Getafe and Cuatro Vientos and at the Carabanchel barracks. Meanwhile General Fanjul, in charge of the overall Insurgent effort in Madrid, hesitated to bring his troops out of the Montaña barracks. Then at 5 a.m. on 19 July in Barcelona, General Fernández Burriel seized the principal squares and public buildings and invited General Goded to fly in from Palma de Majorca to take command in Catalonia. But anarcho-syndicalist workers and Catalan federalists, armed and led

Insurgent volunteers march through Burgos on their departure for the front in southern Spain.

¡ SI NO ES POR ESTOS... !

Above: If Not For These.
Woodcut from an anarchist
publication commemorating
the proletarian defense of
Madrid, 19 July 1936.

Right: makeshift distribution
of arms in Barcelona.

Above: workers manning a barricade erected to defend Barcelona against Insurgent troops.

Below: one of the Assault Guard companies which remained loyal to the government and helped to defeat the insurrection in Barcelona.

Captured by civilians and militiamen, an Insurgent officer is led to summary court martial at the Montaña barracks.

by loyal Assault and Civil Guards, retook the city at a frightful cost in blood. At 5 p.m. a defeated and possibly remorseful General Goded surrendered, and at 7 p.m. he went on the radio to acknowledge defeat and release his followers from further resistance. On Monday the 20th, thousands of semi-armed Madrileños, cheering the recorded broadcast of the Goded surrender speech, stormed the Montaña barracks, lynched a number of the officers found within, captured about 50,000 rifles and a large quantity of ammunition, and marched off to rescue the neighboring cities of Alcalá, Guadalajara and Toledo from the Insurgents.

At the end of four days the Insurgents controlled about one third of Spain, including the most important wheat-growing districts. But they had captured none of Spain's four industrial cities, and they were far from fully controlling a hostile population in Galicia, Asturias and Andalusia. Their triumphs had been due to careful organization, to the ardor of their middle-rank officers, to speed and trick slogans and to the refusal of the Madrid government to arm civilians. Their failures occurred where loyal officers and government officials deprived them of surprise and gave leadership to the ardent defensive efforts of Socialist and anarchist workers. Most serious of all the failures from the immediate strategic standpoint was the outcome of the rising in the navy. On each of the half-dozen seaworthy cruisers, sailors' committees arrested and killed their pro-Insurgent officers and sailed for the Straits of Gibraltar, where they established a blockade which effectively isolated General Franco's Moroccan army from the peninsula.

48

On his first day in Tetuán the General, recognizing that the *pronunciamiento* had fallen short of its goal, sought limited foreign military aid. On 19 July he sent Luis Bolín to Rome to ask for twelve bombers and three fighter planes, and on 22 July, through Colonel Juan Beigbeder, he requested ten transport planes from Germany. Although much has been written about Carlist arms purchases and training missions in Italy, and about the multiple contacts between German and Spanish businessmen and army officers, neither Mussolini nor Hitler had anticipated a civil war in Spain. The Italian dictator made up his mind on 25 July, perhaps partially influenced by the fact that France was going to aid the Republic and that England was unhappy about the French intent. In Germany the Foreign Office and the army both opposed any involvement in a military adventure. But Johannes Bernhardt, a Nazi businessman from Tetuán, and Hermann Goering, commander of the Luftwaffe, convinced Hitler personally on 26 July.

On 20 July, the Republican Prime Minister José Giral had sent an urgent appeal to France, whose Socialist Premier, Léon Blum, immediately agreed to sell Spain some twenty Potez planes, and quantities of small arms and supplies. But on 22 July, in London, Blum discovered that most of the British cabinet were inclined toward the Insurgents. Upon returning to Paris he learned that most of the non-Socialist members of his own cabinet were loath to intervene. The uproar in the French press suggested that the Blum government might well be overthrown if it sent arms to Spain. More important, a weak and divided France could not afford to offend

Parading on deck, the crew of the Spanish cruiser *Miguel de Cervantes* give the Communist salute after arresting their pro-Insurgent officers.

England. Britain had signed a naval agreement with Germany in 1935 and had refused to hear of sanctions when Hitler had unilaterally remilitarized the Rhineland in March 1936. Whatever her sentiments, indeed whatever her strategic concern for the Pyrenean border or for events in Morocco, France had to retain England as the only ally capable of defending her against a resurgent Germany.

The Germans and Italians acted quickly once they had made their decision. Hitler sent twenty Junker Ju-52 transport planes to Seville and Morocco, and on 28 July these planes began airlifting Franco's élite troops across the Straits of Gibraltar. Italy dispatched twelve Savoias-81 bombers, but on 30 July one fell into the sea and two made a forced landing in French Morocco. This direct evidence of Italian intervention renewed the determination of Blum and his Air Minister, Pierre Cot, at least to complete their initially agreed shipment. On 2 August the French proposed that all the major European powers join in a Non-Intervention Agreement. Within the next few days they shipped the Potez planes, and on 8 August they closed the Pyrenean frontier in the hope of gaining quick international cooperation on non-intervention.

The German battleship *Deutschland* called at Ceuta on 3 August. On 5 August the *Usaramo*, escorted by a German torpedo-boat, and unloading at night, delivered six Heinkel He-51 fighter planes with their crews and miscellaneous supplies at Cádiz. On the same day German bombers had put the Republican battle-cruiser *Jaime I* out of action, and a total of perhaps forty Italian and German aircraft were now available to convoy Insurgent troopships across the Straits. At Gibraltar the British practiced a pro-Insurgent neutrality. They refused to supply ships, but passed along information concerning unregistered vessels in Portuguese ports and permitted the Insurgents to use the Gibraltar telephone exchange for communications with Italy, Germany and Portugal. At the same time they refused to sell oil to the Republican navy. In the international city of Tangier the municipal government refused facilities to Republican ships, but placed no obstacles on the transit of men and goods to the Insurgent zone.

Portugal also cooperated with the Insurgents from the outset. Her roads and telephones were available to link the forces of General Mola in Castile with those of General Franco in Andalusia. Franco's brother Nicolás, and the millionaire tobacco-smuggler Juan March, established diplomatic and financial headquarters in Lisbon, and they rather than the Republican ambassador (the distinguished medieval historian Claudio Sánchez Albornoz) were treated as the representatives of Spain. When the Republican navy stopped German freighters approaching Spanish ports, the Salazar government permitted the Germans to unload military equipment in Lisbon and transported that equipment by rail to the Spanish frontier. Although the United States had in 1935 adopted a Neutrality Act embargoing the sale of arms to countries at war, oil had not been listed as a war

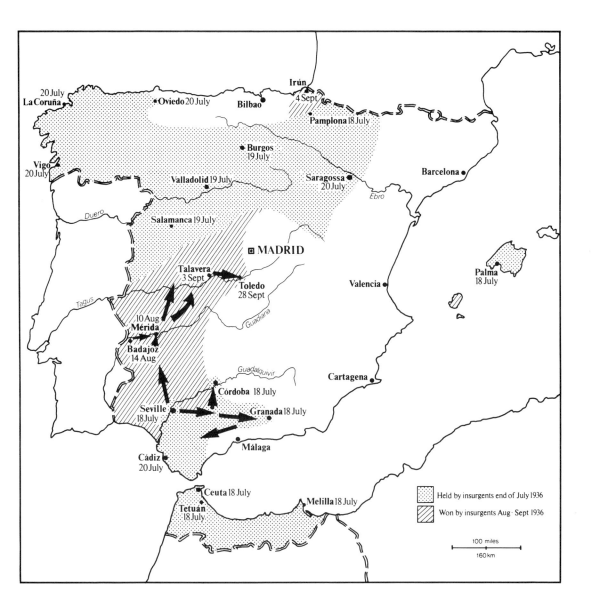

On the map:

La Coruña 20 July
Oviedo 20 July
Bilbao
Irún 4 Sept
Pamplona 18 July
Vigo 20 July
Burgos 19 July
Valladolid 19 July
Saragossa 20 July
Barcelona
Duero
Salamanca 19 July
MADRID
Ebro
Talavera 3 Sept
Toledo 28 Sept
Valencia
Palma 18 July
Tagus
Mérida 10 Aug
Guadiana
Badajoz 14 Aug
Guadalquivir
Cartagena
Córdoba 18 July
Seville 18 July
Granada 18 July
Cádiz 20 July
Málaga
Ceuta 18 July
Melilla 18 July
Tetuán 18 July

Held by insurgents end of July 1936
Won by insurgents Aug–Sept 1936

100 miles
160 km

Map showing the progress of the Insurgent advance toward Madrid, July–September 1936.

commodity under this act. On 18 July some five Texaco tankers were on the high seas, bound for Spain, and Texaco officials decided to direct these tankers to Insurgent-held ports. American oil thus reached the Insurgents early in August.

These several forms of military aid transformed the prospects of the war. Between 18 July and 5 August the best-equipped Insurgent troops were in Morocco, unable to cross the Straits except in small numbers by airplane. General Queipo de Llano held a bridgehead in Seville, and General Mola had marched his enthusiastic, but not very numerous or well-equipped Carlist and Falangist troops to the Somosierra pass north of Madrid. Here they had dug in, and were

Poster issued by the Foreign Ministry of the Republic for distribution in France. The caption reads: 'One dark day, the Castilian peasant, whose son was killed as a soldier in Morocco, found his village square turned into a Moroccan market.'

fighting heroic local actions against proletarian and student militia units sent out from Madrid. But without supplies and transport their advance was completely stalled. When German arms and American oil began to arrive in mid-August, Mola could clean up his rear-guard, establish supply lines and plan for an eventual advance to Madrid.

Similarly, when the forty Italian and German planes had given the Insurgents control of the Straits, Franco's élite troops, some 20,000 Moors and Foreign Legionaries, could be rapidly transported to southern Andalusia. From early August to mid-October the most important fighting occurred in south-western Spain as the army of Africa moved from Seville to Mérida and Badajoz, then up the Tagus valley toward Madrid. They were organized in columns of 500 to 1,000 under Spanish officers: General Varela, Colonels Yagüe and Carlos Asensio, Lieutenant-Colonels Barrón, Delgado and De Tella, Majors Castejón and Mizzian. The officers shared their pride of service in the crack Foreign Legion which had been created largely by General Franco in the 1920s. They carried in their wallets pictures of their comrades killed in Barcelona or at the Montaña barracks. Relations with their own troops were excellent. Officers flying between the front and Melilla wrote and carried letters for the Moorish soldiers, and delivered to their families the rings, gold

Left: drawing by Luis Quintanilla of Moroccan troops plundering and killing.

Below: Moorish soldiers disembark in Spain after being airlifted from North Africa. In the first days of his rebellion, Franco's success depended heavily on these reinforcements.

teeth and watches taken from the corpses of the 'reds.' Each soldier carried a 60-pound pack, 200 cartridges and the curved knife with which he killed the wounded or silently murdered opposing sentries at night.

The columns traveled by truck, living off a countryside far richer than that of the Rif in which they had fought their earlier battles. Operating in a hostile, but militarily disorganized, territory, they would halt their trucks perhaps 100 yards short of a village. The men would dismount and advance cautiously on foot. If there were signs of resistance light artillery would bombard the walls or stone buildings likely to be strongpoints. The town would be entered with bayonets fixed. Loudspeakers (German made, and thought of as magical by both the Moors and the villagers) would order that all doors be opened and white flags displayed. Anyone caught with arms in hand, or with a shoulder bruised by rifle recoil, would be shot. From the viewpoint of the Insurgent officers, not they, but the ununiformed Popular Front militia were the 'rebels,' whose lives were forfeited as such. While their ammunition lasted, and while they enjoyed the cover of the buildings or trees, the militia would fight desperately. Often the army of Africa suffered heavy casualties for its scorn of the enemy, and by mid-August Colonel Yagüe was seeking volunteer reinforcements from Portugal. But whenever they were threatened by a flanking movement, or dislodged by artillery fire, the militiamen would flee in bunches, having no idea of the value of dispersal. Insurgent machine-guns would slaughter them; the corpses would be looted, piled up, sprinkled with petroleum and burned. A platoon would be left behind to assure communications and 'public order.' The column would then drive north to the next objective.

In these naïve early days of the war journalists were allowed to accompany the advancing troops. The approach to Badajoz aroused particular interest. It was the capital of the province in which the largest revolutionary land seizures had occurred, and its capture would enable the Insurgents to link their northern and southern armies. Under the eyes of Portuguese, French and English newsmen, 4,000 militia mounted machine-guns on the city walls and barricaded the gateways through which the trolley tracks ran. The Insurgent engineers dynamited one of the city gates, and the legionaries poured through the gap in order to attack the machine-gun posts from the rear. They absorbed over 100 casualties in 20 seconds, but the survivors wiped out the strongpoint. Inside the city Colonel Yagüe released 380 rightist prisoners and heard tales of the shootings of priests and landlords. Hours later journalists began reporting the mass executions of captured militiamen. The American Jay Allen electrified world opinion with his numerically exaggerated report of 4,000 deaths in the municipal bullring. Colonel Yagüe told a Portuguese reporter that perhaps even 2,000 was a slightly high figure. No one can say with certainty how many men were shot, but

there is abundant evidence, especially in the Portuguese press, that such mass killings took place in other towns besides Badajoz.

The most famous single incident in this three-month campaign was the relief of the besieged Alcázar in Toledo. During the first three days of the rising, Insurgent and Popular Front supporters had fought a savage battle in the narrow winding streets of the medieval city. As the militia gradually gained the upper hand, about 1,000 Civil and Assault Guards, Falangists and a handful of infantry cadets retreated into the great stone fortress overlooking the Tagus river. They took with them a few hundred women and children, many of them the families of known leftists, and under the command of Colonel Moscardó they prepared to withstand siege. The government possessed virtually no heavy guns capable of making an impression on the walls, which were at some points several feet thick. Until 24 August they did no shelling at all, partly for lack of projectiles and fuses, partly because the militia were conscious of the presence inside of their own families. At the end of the month they were firing a single 155 mm. and a few 75 mm. guns and were digging tunnels with the intention of blowing up the cellars in which the besieged garrison and its hostages lived.

On 9 September Lieutenant-Colonel Vicente Rojo, who had been an instructor at the Alcázar military academy and who had several personal friends among the defenders, entered the fort under a flag of truce to try to obtain its surrender, and failing that, the release of the hostages. On the 11th a Madrid priest, Father Vásquez Camarasa, tried to persuade Moscardó to release the women and children. The Colonel sent for one of the women, who in his presence assured the padre that the women of the Alcázar wished to share the fate of their men. Two days later the Chilean ambassador Aurelio Núñez Morgado, dean of the diplomatic corps, came to Toledo for the same purpose and was told that the garrison would listen most respectfully to any message he wished to send them via 'the national government at Burgos.'

The siege of the Alcázar. *Above:* government troops advance toward the citadel. *Right:* militiamen during the last attack, still unsuccessful when the advancing Insurgent troops finally relieved the besieged defenders.

Above: ruins of one of the inner courts. *Left:* General Franco and, on the left, Colonel Moscardó, commander of the besieged stronghold.

No one knew just how many people were inside the Alcázar and what supplies Colonel Moscardó disposed of to feed them. On 3 September the Insurgents had taken the town of Talavera. The militia had fled in their usual disorder, and the road to Madrid seemed to be undefended. General Franco made a personal decision at this point to relieve his comrades in the Alcázar before advancing on the capital. On 18 September the desperate besiegers, realizing that time was no longer on their side, exploded three subterranean mines which did some damage to the building but not to its occupants. By 26 September the Insurgents were camped across the river from the fortress. The majority of the demoralized militia was already retreating toward Madrid. Some hundreds made a desperate stand in the cemetery the next morning. It was drenched with shells and then taken, stone by stone, in personal combat. The troops then moved on to the barracks and the hospital, where the wounded were killed in their beds. Late in the afternoon the famished occupants of the Alcázar emerged into the streets now dominated by the army of Africa. A thin and heavily bearded Colonel Moscardó reported the next day to General Varela: 'Sin novedad' ('All quiet'). The defenders had suffered some eighty casualties in the ten-week siege.

Following the relief of the Alcázar Colonel Moscardó became the personal symbol of the Insurgent cause. His son had been taken hostage by the militia in the first days of the war. According to the story now widely publicized, the militia commander had telephoned the Alcázar, and placed the young man on the phone to explain to his father that he would be shot if the fortress did not surrender. The Colonel told his son to commend his soul to God and to die bravely. Sometime in August the son was executed. The text of the conversation has been printed in many languages on the cellar wall of the Alcázar, today one of the principal monuments of the victorious *Cruzada*. People in Spain still argue about whether such a conversation could have taken place. But factual accuracy in this case is less important than symbolic meaning. In the Spanish Civil War there were fathers on both sides who would have done exactly what Colonel Moscardó testifies that he did; and there were sons who would have died willingly after such an injunction. Speaking more generally, the siege of the Alcázar symbolized for the Insurgents the patriotic and religious purity of a movement which inspired its followers to suicidal heroism. For the Republicans it symbolized their own military incompetence and the Fascist use of hostages.

During the first three months of the war all the European powers established what were to be their consistent attitudes toward the Spanish conflict. The majority of the French people hoped for a Republican victory but were afraid to take any risks which might lead to war with Germany. The majority in the cabinet and in the Chamber of Deputies also sympathized with the Republic. Many prominent Catholics favored the government, largely because the staunchly Catholic Basques were fighting on the Republican side, and many military men whose caste sympathies lay with the Insurgent generals were nevertheless anxious about the threat to French strategic interests in Morocco, the Mediterranean and along the Pyrenean border. Thus, although the border was officially closed on 8 August, frontier police did not seriously try to prevent small arms, volunteers, trucks and petroleum from crossing into Spain. The novelist André Malraux organized what the French government could no longer do while trying to establish non-intervention: namely, the purchase and dispatch of about thirty aircraft in addition to the original twenty Potez planes. All of them were of First World War vintage: Bréguets with a maximum speed of 70 m.p.h., 1918 Nieuports and de Havillands.

The Germans were more systematic and more discreet. They had long desired to expand their Spanish commerce and their Spanish and Moroccan mining investments. But Hitler was primarily concerned with German rearmament and with his plans to absorb Austria and then expand militarily in eastern Europe. He wanted no general European war, and when he gave Goering the green light at Bayreuth on 26 July he undoubtedly thought that the war would be short, that Germany could supply Franco's needs without depleting her own armament, and that she would acquire valuable field experience for German aviators, gunners and communications teams. From August until October freighters equipped with South American flags left Hamburg about every five days. They carried bombers and fighter planes, anti-aircraft and anti-tank guns, trucks, mine- and flame-throwers, field radio stations and telephone

Arms for Anti-Fascist Spain. Poster issued as part of the campaign to persuade the French government to supply the Republic with arms.

Soldiers of the Condor Legion, the units sent by Hitler to Spain to gain practical experience of modern fighting conditions.

switchboards, rifles and machine-guns together with their ammunition. They also carried the pilots, gun crews, radio operators and mechanics who would use this equipment and report on its military effectiveness. Until 28 August German personnel were under strict orders not to take part in actual fighting, and until the assault on Madrid Germany would not publicly acknowledge the presence of Germans with the Insurgent army.

Mussolini, after his few days' hesitation, threw himself enthusiastically into the Spanish adventure. The Italians established an air and naval base on Majorca, supplied several submarines and destroyers to the Insurgents, and by mid-October had sent about twenty whippet tanks to the army which was preparing the attack on Madrid. Mussolini was enjoying the afterglow of his Ethiopian victory. He believed that for reasons of virility and imperial destiny it was important to engage his military forces in another war. Though he had loudly proclaimed his ambition to dominate the Mediterranean, he did not, in these early weeks nor at any time later in the war, demand any specific monetary or territorial reward for his aid.

The Portuguese government was frankly and openly committed from the start. For Antonio Salazar, who had only recently solidified his own reactionary dictatorship, the triumph of the Insurgents was a matter of life and death. He offered troops to Mola on 26 July, and spoke on 1 August of sending the Portuguese army if necessary. His frontier police and military intelligence worked directly with the Insurgents, and on 17 September he announced the formation of the Portuguese Legion which eventually may have supplied as many as 20,000 troops to General Franco.

The Soviet Union spoke out in support of the Republican government, and during August numerous factory mass meetings collected money for food and medical aid to the Republic in what was probably the most genuine manifestation of popular political feeling ever permitted by Josef Stalin. The Soviets also saw in the Spanish Civil War a possible opportunity to achieve practical military and diplomatic cooperation with the Western powers. But they were much too concerned with the threat of German rearmament to jump quickly into a military conflict at the south-western tip of the Continent. Only after the extent of Italian-German-Portuguese intervention was clear to the world did the Soviets warn that they might not remain neutral. In the second half of October six or eight Russian freighters delivered to Spain's Mediterranean ports about 400 trucks, 100 heavy tanks, 50 fighter planes, plane and tank crews and large quantities of food and medical supplies.

British motives were as complex as those of the French. Britain had large investments all over Spain: in the sherry industry, citrus fruits and the Rio Tinto ores of the Insurgent zone; in the Basque mining, steel and shipping industries; and in the electric plants of Catalonia. Britain was also sensitive to the balance of power in the Mediterranean, and hence to events close to Gibraltar and Tangier,

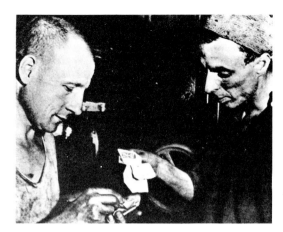

Soviet support for Republican Spain. *Above:* a factory collection. *Left:* a grotesque puppet figure of Franco is carried through Moscow in a demonstration. The slogans read 'Made in Italy' and 'Made in Germany.'

Clement Attlee, leader of the British Labour Party, gives the clenched fist salute during a visit to Madrid. Next to him stands General Miaja, commander of the Republican forces in Madrid.

to the fate of the Spanish navy and to the naval intervention of Italy on behalf of the Insurgents. The Labour Party and the majority of intellectuals were strongly pro-Republican. The City of London, reflecting both the financial anxieties and the conservative political preferences of its investors, was pro-Insurgent. The Baldwin government hoped for a quick, and not too cruel, Insurgent victory, and navy commanders who were politically favorable to Franco allowed political refugees to take asylum in Gibraltar and to board British vessels in Galician ports. The Baldwin government was also determined to improve relations with Germany and Italy, to maintain the traditional alliance with Portugal and to reassure France while restraining Blum's desire to aid the Republic.

The principal aim of both France and England was to keep the Spanish Civil War from becoming a general European war. To this end, in the first days of August, they sponsored the establishment of a Non-Intervention Committee, whose function it would be to keep arms from reaching both sides. By 24 August Germany and Italy had accepted the notion 'in principle.' On 9 September the Committee held its first meeting in London. England, France, Germany, Italy and the Soviet Union were represented, but Portugal had not yet named a delegate. The Spanish government was eager to present evidence of intervention. However, neither the Madrid government nor the Burgos junta had been invited to join the Committee, and one of the first procedural rules adopted was a requirement that allegations could be heard only if presented by a member of the Committee. It was also decided that all charges must be submitted in writing to the accused government and that their answers in writing should be awaited before further discussion ensued.

In desperation the Republicans presented their case before the League of Nations General Assembly on 30 September. This action gave them the opportunity to publicize their evidence, but earned them the enmity of the recently appointed chairman of the Non-Intervention Committee, Lord Plymouth. During October the Committee undertook to examine the Spanish government's charges, which were now sponsored by a Committee member, the Soviet ambassador Ivan Maisky. Most of the evidence referred to incidents before 28 August, the date on which the Fascist powers had committed themselves, albeit with reservations that deprived their pledges of any binding force, not to send war supplies to Spain. The Committee decided it was incompetent to hear the pre-28 August data, and it judged the other data to be insubstantial since it was based principally on newspaper reports. As the Fascist powers and Portugal had all solemnly declared that the charges were without foundation, acceptance of the evidence would have involved branding the accused government as liars.

From the very beginning Lord Plymouth used all procedural devices to protect the Fascist powers. The discussions were dominated by the flamboyant Italian ambassador, Count Dino Grandi. It

While France Sleeps, Germany arms the Insurgents. A Republican cartoonist's view of the armaments situation.

Mientras Francia duerme...
Pendant que dort la France...
While France sleeps...

was always possible for him impudently and elegantly to deny all charges, for the simple reason that there were absolutely no binding clauses in the Non-Intervention Agreement and therefore nothing which could legally be defined as a clear violation. Altogether, the proceedings of the Committee would have been worthy of the talents of a Swift or a Voltaire. Their practical force was to white-wash Fascist aid to the Insurgents while pointing the accusing finger at the Soviets. The latter served notice on 8 October that they would not be more bound than other countries by the Non-Intervention Agreement, and this warning coincided approximately with the loading of the first Russian freighters at Odessa.

By late October, when the Insurgents were approaching the outskirts of Madrid, the *pronunciamiento* of 18 July had become an international civil war. Italy, Germany and Portugal were directly intervening on behalf of General Franco. The Soviet Union was arming the Republic. France and England were divided in their sympathies but anxious that the fighting should not spread beyond the peninsula. In the western hemisphere the Mexican government of Lázaro Cárdenas strongly favored the Republican cause, but was not able to send really effective military aid. In the United States public opinion was predominantly sympathetic to the Republic, but not to the point of wishing to risk military involvement. Throughout Latin America, generally conservative governments favored the Insurgents without intervening in the war.

Spain Has Come Into Her Own! Nationalist poster.

Sons of the People, to the Barricades. Republican poster.

The fervent collectivist revolution carried through in the Republican zone in the first months of the war completely overthrew the established order. One of the worst excesses of the prevailing anticlericalism was the 'execution' by a firing-squad of this monumental statue of Christ in the outskirts of Madrid.

Chapter Four

REVOLUTION AND COUNTER-REVOLUTION

In the weeks following the *pronunciamiento* of 17–20 July that portion of Spain in which the military revolt had been defeated underwent a profound social revolution. The long-repressed hatreds and the messianic hopes of millions of workers and peasants could suddenly be acted upon. Jails were opened, property and legal records were destroyed and churches were burned or converted to entirely secular uses. The overwhelming desire of the moment was to destroy all vestiges of hierarchy and privilege, and to affirm the absolute equality of man. In the cities felt hats and ties, the symbols of bourgeois status, disappeared from the streets. Restaurants and hotels were collectivized and run by their own staffs. Waiters wore white coats, served with the same finesse as before, and charged the same prices – but the clients dined in shirtsleeves and the worker management abolished tipping. Women appeared in trousers, legalized abortion was demanded and information on venereal disease and birth control was freely distributed. The private homes of the wealthy who had fled to France were converted for use as schools, orphanages and free clinics.

In the economic sphere the workers carried out a revolution whose main characteristics were the insistence on local, collective authority, pride of workmanship and absence of technical innovation. This revolution was proportionately strongest in Catalonia, where about 70 per cent of all industry was collectivized between late July and the end of October. Practically all factories employing as many as a hundred workers, and all public utilities – tramways, electricity, gas and water – were collectivized. Apartment buildings were municipalized and rents were lowered, while at the same time wages were raised about 10 per cent. Dairies, slaughter-houses and large urban markets were also collectivized, with a view to eliminating middle-men and lowering the price of food. Retail stores, machine shops and garages were generally not collectivized. Worker committees might check on prices, or might urge metal shops to convert from civilian business to the manufacture of grenades and armor-plate, but they did not try to manage small businesses. Similarly they did not attempt to alter the property arrangements, the cultivation or marketing methods of the farmers who fed the industrial district of Greater Barcelona.

At first the Catalan workers were determined to do everything by themselves. They had defeated the rebellion on 19 July and they had energetically restored production in the last days of July while the regional government was still in a state of shock. Besides which, anarcho-syndicalist doctrine called for the establishment of an egalitarian society in which the great industrial units would be autonomously managed by committees of worker-technicians. The CNT-dominated committees invited those owners and top administrators who had not fled, or been shot, to continue working in their own collectivized plants at salaries which were approximately double the average worker's wage, and the committees took great pride in careful management and in the rapid restoration of production.

Their experience soon led them to appreciate the complexity of an urban industrial economy. The difficulty of obtaining raw materials and replacement parts, and the need to maintain exports, induced in them a readiness to cooperate with the Generalitat, the Catalon regional government. For his part, Luis Companys, the President of the Generalitat, a former labor lawyer and a man of broad human sympathies, was prepared to ratify the actions of the worker committees and to fulfil those social aims which were not incompatible with small business and farmer interests. On 7 August the Generalitat created a War Industries Commission which progressively took over responsibility for the largest collectivized factories, usually at the request of the worker committees. By mid-October the Commission was managing more than 400 plants and throughout the year 1937 it managed about 500 factories employing over 50,000 workers. Banks were reopened and at least until well into 1937 continued normal savings, commercial and investment operations. The regional government also reached an early accord with the British Consulate for the protection of some 87 British-owned firms in Barcelona. Noting the clear tendency of anarcho-syndicalist factory committees to husband their financial resources and their stocks of raw material, to follow perfectly traditional technical and administrative methods and to cooperate with a 'bourgeois' government, the press of the Left-Marxist POUM (Partido Obrero de Unificación Marxista) began to refer ruefully to 'syndical capitalism.'

Similar processes took place in the other principal urban centers, with the important exception of Bilbao. In Valencia about half of all industry was collectivized and in Madrid about 30 per cent. In the Mediterranean ports all public utilities and dock facilities were collectivized and then managed by mixed CNT-UGT committees. In the Asturian mining towns the more radical traditions of October 1934

CAMPE/INO!
ENTREGANDO *tus* NARANJA/ *al* CLUEA APLA/TA/ FA/CI/MO *al*

pepe

were renewed. The committees collectivized all commerce, abolished the use of money for local purposes, calculated wages in kind according to the size of family rather than to work accomplished, and set up public kitchens where they served meals in exchange for chits. The fishermen of Avilés and Gijón collectivized their equipment, the docks and the canning factories. As grain and meat supplies rapidly dwindled, the northern provinces depended increasingly on the distribution by barter of the coastal fishing catch.

Throughout the rural areas of Popular Front territory, a corresponding revolution took place, yet one which varied greatly from village to village. Once again, social equality and local control were the guiding impulses, rather than any organized conception of the new society to be created. Almost everywhere rents were abolished and property records burned. In some instances (more frequently in the dry, sparsely populated parts of New Castile, La Mancha and Aragon) the entire village land was collectivized, while in others the land belonging to absent owners was distributed among the peasant majority. Sometimes the confiscated land was collectivized while other property relations remained untouched. In some villages no property changes occurred. Almost everywhere the former municipal governments were replaced by committees including one member for each party in the Popular Front. In some cases this meant little

Left: Luis Companys, President of the autonomous Catalan government and the eloquent spokesman of the Catalan Left-Liberal party, the Esquerra.

Right: Countrymen! Deliver your oranges and help to crush fascism. Republican poster campaigning for greater agricultural productivity.

change – if, for example, the former *alcalde* (mayor) had been a Socialist or a Left-Republican, he would simply become head of the village committee and continue business as before. However, where the CEDA or the Lliga Catalana had won the February elections, the *alcalde* and the Civil Guards would probably have fled or been imprisoned or assassinated, and new men dominated the committees.

Generally speaking, methods of work were not changed, but in some villages of the Castilian *meseta* young Socialist committeemen managed to overcome historic peasant opposition to the introduction of harvesting machines. Though many of the estates of absentee landlords were confiscated, the land was not redistributed, but continued to be cultivated by a local committee instead of by a steward representing the landowner. Thus in the summer of 1936 production was not upset by the revolution, but neither was there much initiative toward a change in existing economic practices. The committees controlled wages and the sale of the harvest. They converted the church, whose altar had frequently been burned in the first days, into a market, or, if close to the front, a hospital. They requisitioned the services of the local doctors and druggists, and thousands of peasants now received some kind of medical attention for the first time in their lives, without charge to the patient. They also collectivized barber shops and the retail trade in canned goods. As a result many peasants received their first professional haircuts and tasted their first canned fruit.

Some villages, usually those in isolated mountainous areas where there had been minimal contact with the outside world, abolished money and declared a 'republic' within their municipal boundaries. The anarchist peasants considered money second only to the Church as a source of corruption. In Catalonia long traditions of commerce kept them from going to excessive lengths, but in Aragon, New Castile, Murcia and Andalusia, dozens of villages proudly abolished the use of money and conducted all local commerce by chits or barter. Wages were revised in accordance with the number of a man's dependents rather than the skill or quantity of his work. Money, still a necessary evil in dealing with the outside world, was confiscated by the committee and given to the villagers for specific purchases or travel needs.

These varied urban and rural revolutions were accompanied by varying degrees of terror. In Madrid the CNT, the UGT and the Communist Party all had their lists of suspected 'Fascists' and 'saboteurs.' They established joint purge committees to try the suspects, and although there was a heavy presumption of guilt, especially if the same name appeared on all three lists, they usually tried to find real evidence, and a person who had the presence of mind to prove his innocence or expose a false informer might be treated to a round of drinks and given a guard of honor to return home. But the city was also plagued by gangs of juvenile delinquents who requisitioned automobiles, gave themselves dramatic titles such as the 'Lynxes,'

Propaganda for the Republican National Guards
shows a guardsman stamping bossism,
reaction and crime into their grave.

the 'Red Lions,' the 'Death Battalion' and the 'Godless,' and who
may have murdered well over a thousand people during the first
three months of the war.

While in Madrid the revolutionary organizations generally
cooperated with each other, in the other main cities their mutual
rivalries were an important element in the terror. In Barcelona
several prominent labor leaders died as a result of UGT-CNT warfare
on the waterfront. The Left-Communist, and partially Trotskyite
POUM, and the Communist-dominated PSUC (Partido Socialista
Unificado de Cataluna), directed their fire at one another as well as
at the reactionary bosses. In Valencia and Málaga the internecine
warfare of UGT, CNT and Communist factions resulted in a number
of deaths. Prison raids were another important aspect of the urban
terror. On 23 August, after a mysterious fire in Madrid's Model
Prison, the guards decided on their own to shoot fourteen prominent political prisoners, among them a conservative Republican
deputy, two founders of the Falange and several officers who had
taken part in the Madrid rising. The new government under José
Giral had had no intention whatsoever of executing these men. On
several occasions in cities in the Republican zone dozens of political
prisoners were lynched in reprisal for Insurgent air or naval raids.

The widespread village revolutions were also accompanied by varying degrees of terror. In southern Spain particularly, priests and Civil Guards were always shot if they had sided with the Insurgents; occasionally they were shot even if they had made no move on 18 July. Throughout the Popular Front zone the village committees acted on their own initiative, and generalization concerning the results is impossible. Some villages took pride in deciding not to shoot any 'class enemies' at all, but to 're-educate' them as long as they did not sabotage the revolution. Some committees warned the priest and the landlord to leave for a time at least, lest uncontrollable elements lynch them. Some villages shot the priest, the Civil Guards, the main landlords and professional men such as notaries and pharmacists, known or assumed to favor the old order. In villages with populations of several thousand, the death toll might run between four or five and thirty-five to forty, with the casualties tending to be higher in Andalusia and the south-east than in Valencia and Catalonia. Sometimes the executions were carried out by the local committees, sometimes by outside militia squads. In Aragon the Durruti column (led by the famous anarchist Buenaventura Durruti), on its way toward Saragossa, earned an evil reputation among the conservative peasants. On the other hand there are also testimonials to the intervention of Durruti personally to prevent the killing of landlords who had not aided the rising, but who had been condemned simply as known Catholics or monarchists. Frequently the crudest revolutionaries felt an almost superstitious respect for doctors and teachers, and they spared many such even when the individuals in question had engaged actively in reactionary politics.

The practical results of the collectivizations also varied too greatly to permit of accurate generalization. Where raw materials continued to be available, where workers were proud and skilful in the maintenance of their machines or tools, where a reasonable proportion of the technical personnel sympathized with the revolution, and where committees left the technical decisions to the experts, factories operated successfully. Where materials ran short, where replacement parts could not be found (or were hoarded), where UGT-CNT rivalries embittered the workers and placed political considerations ahead of operating efficiency, the collectivized factories failed. Similarly in the countryside – there were collectives where machines were intelligently used and human problems tactfully handled; and there were collectives where the absence of intelligent direction led to the demoralization of the peasants and to greatly reduced production. In the villages where money had been abolished there were committees which showed great acumen in the sale of the harvest and distributed money for all reasonable outside expenses; there were committees which used their power to prevent the sale of tobacco, liquor and 'indecent' or 'politically harmful' literature; and there were committees which simply burned or stole the cash resources of their village. The common denominator of all these situations was the energy with which the common people formed committees, gladly substituted for a central authority they had rarely respected, and ran their own affairs along collectivist and egalitarian lines. It was a phenomenon which had occurred before in Spanish history, notably during the resistance to Napoleon, in the Carlist communities during the 1830s, and in the 'cantonalist' and 'federalist' revolts of 1873.

The collectivist revolution was at its height during the first three months of the war. Indeed the anarchists, the anti-Stalinist Communists of the POUM and most of the Left-Socialists felt that the Civil War would not be worth fighting unless that spontaneous revolution were to be protected and later extended. But the practical exigencies of the situation placed the revolution almost immediately on the defensive. If Catalonia was the heartland of anarcho-syndicalism it was also populated by a tenacious urban middle class and by hard-headed property-loving peasants. In early August the other revolutionary parties had forced the PSUC not to join the middle-class regional government. On 6 September Andrés Nin, the leading theoretician of the POUM and a one-time secretary to

Armored car painted with the initials of the Workers' Party of Marxist Unity, largely destroyed by the Stalinist Unified Socialist–Communist Party of Catalonia (PSUC) following the internecine fighting in Barcelona in May 1937.

CNT

JUNTA DELEGADA DE DEFENSA
DE MADRID

DELEGACION DE PROPAGANDA Y PRENSA

FAI

lo primero es
GANAR la GUERRA

E·218·1937

Leon Trotsky, had proclaimed that the dictatorship of the proletariat existed in Barcelona (via the committees, and *outside* the government). But on 17 September he accompanied Luis Companys to Lérida in quest for support from the Generalitat, and on 25 September the CNT and the POUM entered the regional government, with Nin serving as Minister of Justice!

Meanwhile the PSUC in Catalonia, and the Communist Party in Valencia, had come forward to defend the prosperous commercial farmers of Catalonia and Valencia against unwanted collectivization. And where locally autonomous collectives had been established in the interior, the Communists advocated 'nationalization' rather than 'collectivization,' since the former would imply that the collectives' activities were subject to central governmental supervision. For the Communist Party, and for the right-wing Socialists and the Republicans who now accepted their lead, the most important task was to win the war, not to make a social revolution. Winning the war would require rebuilding the authority of the central government, pleasing the Soviets (who in early October had decided to send military aid) and eventually persuading France and England to help the Republic. To allay the fears of the capitalist democracies it was necessary to curb the revolution, and to please Stalin it was necessary to eliminate the POUM. Soviet freighters received orders not to unload in anarchist- and Trotskyite-tainted Barcelona, and on 17 December Nin resigned his post in the Catalan government.

In Madrid also the revolutionary forces were placed on the defensive after the opening weeks of the war. It was necessary first to curb the terrorism which threatened rapidly to discredit the Republic in the eyes of world democratic opinion. The government broadcast radio warnings to the people not to open their doors at night to unidentified strangers. It permitted, and in some cases privately encouraged, persons who felt threatened to take refuge in foreign embassies, and it allowed several embassies to rent extra buildings for the purpose of sheltering political refugees. It established 'Popular Tribunals' under professional judges and lawyers to provide some degree of orderly legal procedure and defense rights in the investigation of accused 'Fascists.' The Socialist leader Indalecio Prieto went on the air on 10 August to condemn political assassination and to insist that the Republic should not imitate the horrors taking place in the Insurgent zone. On 23 August, after the lynchings in the Model Prison, he began another broadcast with the flat statement: 'Today we have lost the war.' At the same time the Giral government did not interfere with the numerous collectivizations occurring in Madrid's predominantly small-scale industries. It hoped rather to capitalize on the enthusiasm and initiative of the UGT and CNT workers, and to postpone for the postwar era all permanent decisions about property.

The victory at the Montaña barracks and the successful defense of the Somosierra pass by worker and student militia units had created

Opposite: The first task is to win the war. Poster issued by the Madrid defense junta canvassing for unity among the anarchist National Confederation of Labor, the Anarchist Federation of Spain and the Communist Party.

Largo Caballero, who as Prime Minister from September 1936 to May 1937 brought temporary unity to the Republican factions in the struggle against the Nationalists.

an unrealistic euphoria at the end of July. This mood was succeeded by an equally unrealistic defeatism in August as the army of Africa swept through Extremadura and as thousands of terror-stricken peasant refugees crowded into the capital. It was clear that a government of middle-class liberals could not galvanize the latent energies of the masses or create the military discipline necessary to defend the capital against professional troops.

On 4 September the Left-Socialist Francisco Largo Caballero became Prime Minister. He was a plasterer, a man of proletarian origin and life style, a longtime trade union official, a labor counselor of the Primo de Rivera government and Minister of Labor in the first Republican cabinet. As head of the UGT he commanded the loyalty of organized labor, and as a recent convert to revolutionary socialism he was the idol of the militant workers and students. He had been the colleague of both monarchist and Republican ministers, and even his enemies acknowledged his personal integrity. He was able to chair a government consisting of liberal Republicans, Socialists of both Right and Left and Communists. He was respected by the minority of professional military men who had remained loyal to the Republic, and he cooperated (at this time) with the Communist Party, whose newly organized 'Fifth Regiment' was the best-disciplined unit of the popular army. The anarchists also accepted his leadership, and on 4 November they joined his second cabinet.

For the sworn enemies of the Republic the evolution of the Barcelona and Madrid governments during the autumn of 1936 confirmed the 'red' domination of Republican Spain. In appearance, the revolutionaries were taking power, just as the most excitable spokesmen of both Right and Left had said they would after the electoral success of the Popular Front. In fact, the entry of the revolutionary parties into the governments signalized the retreat of the revolution. It meant that the POUM and the CNT had recognized the need to cooperate with the democratic middle class and peasantry to prevent the triumph of a right-wing military dictatorship. It meant that Left-Socialists must also, like their revered chief, postpone the Socialist revolution in favor of saving the democratic Republic. As for the Communists, their avowed aim was to create the unity of all 'democratic' forces, which in the present context meant defending the middle class and prosperous peasants against a 'premature' or 'infantile leftist' revolution.

In the Insurgent zone, from 18 July onward, a very thorough counter-revolution was taking place. Its main traits were the reinforcement of traditional hierarchies, the maintenance of the existing social and economic structure, an official terror supervised by the military and an unofficial terror carried out principally by the Falange and the Carlists. The first act of the military authorities everywhere was to declare the *estado de guerra* (martial law). This meant that the military commander in every city and province became the unquestioned arbiter of civilian as well as military matters. It constituted in effect a disavowal of the principle of civilian supremacy which had been one of the main aims of the

Armed peasants escorting a Church procession in the Insurgent zone, which in the first months of the war underwent a revival of conservative orthodoxy and traditional religious observance.

Republic of 1931. Strikes were forbidden. The Republican land reform (and of course the revolutionary land seizures of 1936) were both nullified. Businesses were obliged to remain open regardless of the sentiments of their owners. Wages and prices were frozen, and semi-voluntary committees of business and professional men were appointed to manage the economy of the Insurgent zone. Under martial law everyone had to obey the authorities or face court-martial. Most priests, civil servants and businessmen cooperated with varying degrees of enthusiasm. Most farmers obeyed out of habit or fear, and those who did not tried to flee to the Republican zone.. Labor leaders, CNT and UGT members and militiamen were herded into emergency prisons, and were by definition liable to be shot for 'military rebellion.'

There were three leading figures among the Insurgent military. General Mola had planned the rising, and he controlled the northern territories seized during the *pronunciamiento*. But he was not highly respected as a soldier, and his position during the early weeks was very precarious due to lack of supplies. General Queipo de Llano, a spiritual descendant of the Cid or of the Italian *condottiere*, carved out a semi-independent principality in Andalusia. He requisitioned transport, arms and capital by the simple threat of the death penalty. He also showed canny business instinct in assuring the continuous export of sherry, olives and citrus fruits. He thereby earned the admiration of the English business community and maintained the

General Mola, as satirized by Luis Quintanilla, and a cartoon issued by the Madrid defense junta of General Franco as crusader for Fascism.

S.E. *el generalisimo*

Caricature of General Queipo de Llano, who governed Andalusia by a combination of crude radio propaganda and massive terror.

flow of foreign exchange to the Insurgent treasury. He established connections with Lisbon for overland commerce and came to rapid understandings for the import of Fiat motors and German chemicals. Loyal followers received the necessary import licenses, and everyone remembered to contribute generously to the chief's personally administered 'charities' and to praise his colorful radio talks. He threatened the 'lily-livered reds' with castration, posted his baggy-trousered Moors in the main squares of Seville and smilingly advised the workers to put on the *salvavida* (life-jacket) – that is, the blue shirt of the Falange.

But the most illustrious Insurgent leader was unquestionably General Francisco Franco, creator of the Foreign Legion, youngest general ever named in the Spanish army and Chief of Staff before the electoral victory of the Popular Front. Spain's wealthiest business-men, the English and German backers of the rising and the majority of Franco's fellow-officers all agreed in thinking of him as the pre-destined leader of a new military dictatorship. A number of high-ranking officers had formed a 'junta' at Burgos on 24 July, but the rapid approach of the Insurgent army toward Madrid, and the hier-archical traditions of the military, made it imperative to form a more substantial government. On 29 September the junta adopted a decree naming Franco 'Head of the Government' and of military operations. On 1 October General Franco promulgated his first Law, in which he referred to himself as 'Head of the State.' Few persons dwelt upon the slight change of phraseology, though General Mola and a few others protested vehemently in private. The observant were put on notice concerning General Franco's limitless ambition, and with his brother Nicolás as principal civilian aide, he continued in all docu-ments to refer to himself as 'Head of the State' – if not by the choice

General Francisco Franco takes the oath of office on his proclamation as 'Head of the State' at Burgos, 1 October 1936.

of his peers, then as he later engraved it on Spanish coins, *por la gracia de Dios* (by the grace of God).

The counter-revolution was everywhere imposed by terror, both official and unofficial. In the towns surrounding Seville the Popular Front authorities had responded to Queipo's seizure of the city by arresting priests and landlords. In some such cases the Insurgent authorities later shot the entire town council, although the released prisoners had testified to the incoming soldiers that they had not been mistreated. Officers, troubled by having priests intercede for the lives of 'reds,' would order the town leaders executed before anyone had time to reach them with a plea. In Castile the population was generally more docile than in Andalusia, but a similar system of terror prevailed under military auspices. Village purge committees normally consisted of the priest, a Civil Guard and a leading landlord. Condemnation of a suspect by all three meant death. In cases of disagreement a lesser penalty would be imposed. But the prisons were overcrowded, and inadequately guarded. Night after night squads of Falangists and Civil Guards visited the jails, called out by list ten, fifteen, perhaps twenty prisoners, put them in trucks, drove to the outskirts of town and massacred them. A particular Falange death signature was a shot between the eyes. The bodies would be left on the highway so as to be seen by everyone traveling to and from

work the following day. Sanitary services placed notices in the press calling for the aid of all doctors and pharmacists to help bury the corpses, and reminding the public not to place graves near wells. General Mola addressed a peremptory telegram to the authorities at Valladolid, ordering them to choose less conspicuous spots for the executions and to bury the dead more rapidly. On 25 September the civil governor of the province published a letter in *El Norte de Castilla*. Referring to the sad necessity for the organs of military justice to carry out death penalties, and granting that the executions were legally open to the public, he nevertheless reminded his readers that their presence at such acts 'says very little in their favor and the considering as a spectacle the mortal torment of a fellow human being, however justified, gives a poor impression of the culture of a people.' In this letter and in press notices appearing in October in Galicia, officials deplored particularly the presence of women and small children.

The counter-revolutionary purges were also characterized by hatred of intellectuals, automatically considered by activists to be leftist sexual perverts. The most famous victim of this type of thinking was the world-famous Granadan poet and dramatist Federico García Lorca, who was arrested on 16 August and assassinated on the night of 18-19 August. Both actions were arranged by members of

Insurgent troops patrol a village near Córdoba, insensible to the anguished pleas for the lives of prisoners taken during the advance.

81

André Masson, *The Satisfied Priest*, a savage attack on the Church's intimate links with the Insurgent cause.

Opposite: sketch by Luis Quintanilla of the Civil Guard, licensed slaughterers of their intellectual and political opponents.

Catholic Action and the Falange, and both occurred with the full knowledge of the Insurgent civil governor. The poet was shot for being the brother-in-law of the Socialist mayor of Granada, for being a friend of the 'Jew' Fernando de los Ríos, for being the writer of 'immoral' plays such as *Yerma*, an alleged homosexual and the author of sarcastic allusions to the Civil Guard and to the conquest of Granada by Ferdinand and Isabella.

Everywhere in Spain intellectuals and doctors were thought of as being politically leftist. Particularly in Galicia and Andalusia, where the Insurgents well knew that the majority of the population was hostile, they shot teachers and physicians. In Carlist Pamplona the festival of the Virgen del Sagrario was celebrated on 15 August along with the mass executions. Late in the afternoon two firing squads, one composed of Falangists and one of Carlists, took a group of fifty to sixty prisoners from the city jail. Most of the captives were Catholics, and several priests were brought along. The victims were handcuffed and hobbled, but not tied together in a single chain. Thus they had relative privacy for their confessions and the squads waited

impatiently for the unusually long confessions to be completed. As the first victims were shot, a hysterical panic seized the remainder. Men tried to run, only to be gunned down like animals. With darkness falling, the Falange and the Carlists quarreled violently, the former shouting that the 'reds' didn't deserve a chance to confess, the latter insisting on the opportunity for practicing Christians to make their peace with God. To settle the matter the priests gave mass absolution to the remainder, the executions were finished, and the trucks regained Pamplona in time for the members of the firing squads to join the procession entering the cathedral.

Equally macabre scenes occurred on the island of Majorca. An Italian Fascist functionary calling himself 'Count Rossi' arrived by air a few days after the rising and removed from office the military governor left behind by General Goded when the latter had flown to Barcelona. Rossi drove his own racing car, wore a black shirt decorated with a white cross, confided to society ladies in Palma that he needed at least one woman a day, and announced the 'crusade' in the villages, flanked by the mayor and the priest. The French Catholic novelist Georges Bernanos had been a longtime resident of the island. He was first shocked by the ferocity of the blood purge and then incensed when he realized the complicity of the Church hierarchy. Describing his experiences in *Les grands cimetières sous la lune*, he referred vitriolically to 'the personage whom convention obliges me to name the Archbishop of Majorca.'

Certain elements were common to the terror in both zones. Both anarchists and professional officers could 'kill without hate,' convinced that their enemies were not human in the same sense as themselves, ready also to sacrifice freely their own lives and often those of their families. Among less exalted participants envy was a powerful motive. Revolutionary and Insurgent purge committees, if at all scrupulous in their operations, were constantly discovering the wildest accusations based on pure spite against a business competitor or a rival in love. Juvenile delinquency flourished in both zones. What could be more thrilling to neurotic teenagers than to drive requisitioned cars, and kill without any sense of remorse, in the name of a 'surgical operation' to cleanse society of a 'gangrenous member?' But while such activities in the Republican zone took place in spite of governmental efforts, in the Insurgent zone they were generally approved by the highest authorities and always at the least condoned. A few theologians offered doctrinal justifications of the *paseo* (political assassination). The magazine *Mundo Hispánico* spoke of purging the rear areas *a cristazo limpio*, with a blow of the crucifix, as fanatical priests had sometimes finished off the Liberal wounded in the Carlist War. The purge must also eradicate the *semilla*, the seeds of Marxism and laicism. It was sarcastically referred to as the *reforma agraria* whereby the *rojoseparatistas*, the 'red' separatists, received finally their piece of land. Had he been able to revisit the earth in the summer and fall of 1936, the Greek tragedian Euripides would have seen armed bands like those in his *Bacchae* ravaging Spain: self-intoxicated fanatics murdering their presumed enemies with the illusion that they were performing a cleansing operation of religious purity. In the Popular Front zone their crimes went far to discredit the entire Republic. In the Insurgent zone their activities contributed greatly toward establishing the unquestioned authority of the military leaders over a largely hostile population.

They shall not pass. Woodcut by the Hungarian artist Ernö Berda, 1939.

MADRID 1936

¡NO PASARAN! ¡PASAREMOS!

Chapter Five

THE SIEGE OF MADRID

Until the relief of the Alcázar on 28 September 1936, and indeed until the artillery fire of the approaching Insurgent army could be heard in the city on 15 October, the general population of Madrid seemed to be unaware of an imminent military assault, and the government even of the beloved trade union chieftain Largo Caballero seemed unable to mobilize for the defense of the capital. There had been much talk of establishing trench and barbed-wire defenses to the west of the city, but the wire and the shovels expected from Catalonia had not arrived, and the Prime Minister felt unable to oblige UGT and CNT building-workers to leave their paid civilian jobs in order to build fortifications.

The only systematic preparations for the defense of Madrid were undertaken by the Communist Party in cooperation with the recently unified Communist-Socialist youth organization. The party had grown from about 10,000 to 50,000 members between February and July, and the unified youth (Juventud Socialista Unificada, or JSU) numbered perhaps 150,000. The strength of both groups was heavily concentrated in Madrid, and the principal JSU leaders were young associates of Largo Caballero who were moving toward the Communist Party and who expected to bring the Left-Socialist chief into full cooperation with the party. They recognized the need for military training and discipline, and they counted upon eventual Soviet military aid despite the fact that the Soviet Union had joined the Non-Intervention Committee.

At the end of July the formation of a 'Fifth Regiment' was announced (there being four regiments normally stationed in Madrid). The Fifth Regiment asked the Giral government for arms and for professional officers to train the volunteer recruits. Some 500 career officers were available in Madrid, but were little trusted by the revolutionary youth. The party therefore introduced the system which had made it possible for the Red Army in 1918 to use the services of Tsarist officers, namely the assignment of political

Opposite: They shall not pass! We shall pass! This photomontage by John Heartfield (the exiled German Communist propagandist) expresses the hope and defiance invested in the battle for Madrid by opponents of Fascism in Spain and all over Europe.

commissars to indoctrinate the soldiers and to guard against any potential counter-revolutionary activity on the part of the officers. The first political commissar of the Fifth Regiment was the Italian Communist Vittorio Vidal, known as Carlos Contreras.

The Fifth Regiment numbered almost 8,000 at the end of July, and about 15,000 by early September. Its columns set an example of firm discipline and relatively sophisticated tactics in the small-scale fighting against General Mola's Falangist and Carlist troops entrenched near the Somosierra pass north of Madrid. Many other columns of a few hundred men each were formed in eager imitation and rivalry of the Fifth Regiment: the 'Galán,' 'Mangada' and 'Perea' columns (named after the leftist professional officers who led them) and such symbolically named units as the 'Union of Proletarian Brothers,' the 'Steel and Sappers,' the 'Maxim Gorki' and the 'Pancho Villa' columns.

In October the Insurgent armies converged toward Madrid on a long arc from the north-west to the south-west. They were advancing more slowly than they had during August and September. The army of Africa had suffered heavy casualties and needed rest after the swift march from Seville to Talavera and Toledo. The attack on a city of over a million population would demand far more supplies, and more coordinated maneuvering, than anything which had been required in the Andalusian and Extremaduran battles. Nevertheless, the Insurgent leadership was supremely confident of taking the city

Shouldering dummy rifles, young Communists parade through the streets of Madrid.

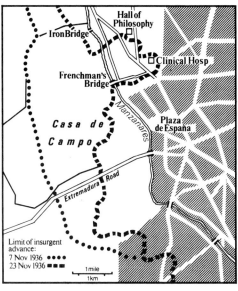

early in November, and was spurred on particularly by intelligence reports of Soviet arms and technicians arriving in the Mediterranean ports.

The first minor air strikes against the capital occurred on 7 October. By the middle of the month troops had occupied all the towns within fifteen miles of Madrid, thereby inundating the city with a flood of refugees and making it necessary to ration food and water. The southern flanks of the invaders were being harassed by largely anarchist guerrilla units operating in the mountains south of the Tagus river, but the invading army could easily control all flat country. Whatever militia units opposed their march were brought to the front in trucks. The Popular Front soldiers did not know how to spread out in open country, advance or retreat as coordinated units. By superiority of numbers, and sheer courage, they might overrun an enemy position; but when machine-guns were turned on them (the Insurgents always enjoyed superior firepower in these engagements) they would bunch up and run for their trucks. Knowing this, the Insurgent machine-gunners could mow them down by the dozens, and sometimes by the hundreds. In the mountainous or forested areas the contest was more equal. Mola was unable to advance from the sierra, and he was obliged to develop a healthy respect for small units operating in the forests near Chapineria.

On 20 October the Republican general José Asensio attacked the invaders' flank near Illescas, but was unable to hold his initial gains. The failure led to his replacement as commander of the central army by General Sebastián Pozas, who was also more friendly to the Communists. On 28 October some forty Russian tanks punctured the Insurgent lines near Illescas, shot up several Moorish-held villages,

Maps showing the Nationalist advance on Madrid October–November 1936 and the ground fought over during the battle for the city, 8–18 November.

89

then had to retreat when the Fifth Regiment troops were unable to keep up with the advancing tanks. But these tactical failures had the important results of forcing General Mola to abandon any thought of outflanking Madrid from the south and to leave a substantial number of combat troops to guard his right flank.

By late October the Insurgents had decided to make their main assault through the Casa de Campo and the University City, and General Mola was announcing that he expected to celebrate the anniversary of the Bolshevik Revolution (7 November) in the capital. The invading army numbered about 25,000, of whom 5,000 would be available for the main attack. On 3 November the defending militia failed in another attack on Mola's right flank. On 4 November his troops took the village and airport of Getafe. Anarchist troops had been hurriedly placed there in shallow, straight trenches which had been dug by women and children from Madrid. Insurgent planes had bombed and machine-gunned the defenders, and the demoralized survivors, along with thousands of peasant refugees, had choked the roads leading into the capital.

Also on 4 November Largo Caballero had broadened the composition of his cabinet, adding four anarchist ministers to the existing coalition of Republicans, Socialists and Communists. Convinced himself that Madrid could not be held, the Prime Minister now decided to evacuate the government to Valencia. On the afternoon of 6 November he appointed as the supreme commander of the city's defense a general who had never been a distinguished field officer, but who was known as a lifelong Republican, José Miaja. The latter was momentarily furious, supposing that he had been selected for the unenviable task of surrendering the city. But in a late night meeting with a few dozen loyal professional officers and with representatives of the Fifth Regiment and the several independent columns, he took the lead in transforming a fatalistic and confused city into an impregnable redoubt. Under the direction of Colonel Vicente Rojo Lluch and Major Manuel Matallana Gómez, the civilian population threw up barricades, organized soup-kitchens, first-aid stations and local message centers. Fifteen to twenty thousand poorly armed troops occupied trenches which had been feverishly dug in the preceding twenty-four hours. Miaja told their officers that there was only one general order, to resist, and when asked where to retreat if necessary, he answered with the sardonic humor for which he became famous, and beloved, 'to the cemetery.'

Caballero's decision to transfer the government to Valencia had given the loyal military officers, the trade union militias, and the Fifth Regiment an unhampered opportunity to conduct the defense of Madrid. Through the momentary dismantling of governmental authority, it also gave an opportunity for barbaric political reprisals. The government had left orders that the political prisoners in the Model Prison be evacuated to Valencia. The Minister of the Interior, Angel Galarza, himself a member of the Caballero wing of the

Enrique Lister, Communist chief of the crack Lister battalion, and General José Miaja, supreme commander of the forces defending Madrid, with a captured Falangist banner.

Opposite: Republican troops man a hastily dug trench on the Madrid front.

You shall not pass. Poster issued by anarchist organizations.

An International Brigade column marches through the streets of Madrid. Eight to ten thousand such troops played a critical role in halting the Insurgent advance.

Socialist Party, had never established full control of the prison guards, most of whom also counted themselves partisans of Largo Caballero. With the capital apparently about to fall, they interpreted the evacuation orders in their own fashion. On two successive nights, 6 and 7 November, they removed nearly 1,000 inmates to Paracuellos de Jarama and Torrejón (villages lying north-east of Madrid) where they had prepared wide trenches. They drove their 'Fifth Column' prisoners to the mass graves and slaughtered them on the spot.

On 6 November the invading army had crossed the unforested western portions of the Casa de Campo. That night, the UGT and CNT marched their members silently into the field to pick up the weapons, and take the positions, of their dead comrades. On the 7th the invaders were slowed down by militia fighting hand to hand among the trees in the eastern part of the park. In the apartment buildings of the south-western suburbs whole companies of Moors died in floor-to-floor assaults. On the invaders' northern flank, the Galán and Barceló columns counter-attacked, and in the south Fifth Regiment troops under Enrique Lister counter-attacked at Villaverde. At 9 p.m. an Italian tank was blown up on the Extremadura road. On the body of one of the officers killed was a copy of General Varela's operational order for the conquest of Madrid. Originally it had been intended for the 7th, but owing to stiffening resistance it had been postponed to the 8th. Colonel Rojo, judging that the order was too complex to be altered at the last minute, moved all his best troops to the Casa de Campo and the University where, according to the captured order, the main assault would take place.

On the morning of 8 November telegrams arrived in the War Ministry congratulating General Franco on his victorious entry. (Descriptions of this entry had already been published in the Portuguese press.) In the streets of Madrid people were chanting the slogans, 'No pasarán' ('They shall not pass,' made famous at the French defense of Verdun in 1916) and 'Madrid shall be the tomb of Fascism.' On the twenty-mile fighting front began the supreme test

They shall not pass! Fascism desires to conquer Madrid. Madrid shall be the tomb of Fascism.

of wills between Generals Varela and Miaja, between the élite army of Africa and the aroused people of Madrid. Wave after wave of Varela's troops braved the machine-gun fire of desperate defenders who had only limited ammunition but who knew exactly where to expect their enemies. German planes bombed the University in preparation for the infantry assault while Varela's men fought their way up the Garabitas heights from which they would be able to observe and shell the city.

As on the 7th, forward patrols reached each of the main bridges over the Manzanares river but were unable to cross. Colonel Rojo had ordered the unarmed reserves to wait under cover, and as hundreds of militia died at their posts, replacements came forward to pick up their rifles. When the Moroccans broke through in the direction of the Model Prison, General Miaja himself drove to the threatened sector, drew out his pistol, and shouted at the retreating soldiers: 'Cowards, die in your trenches, die with your general.' The gap was closed and the Moroccan vanguard decimated while Colonel Rojo dragged Miaja back into the relative safety of his car.

On the afternoon of Sunday, 8 November, the first units of the newly formed International Brigades appeared in Madrid. About

The battle for Madrid. *Above:* ruins of the University City, chief battleground during the siege. *Below:* the aftermath of street fighting.

Mined by Republican forces, Nationalist barracks explode, killing a large
number of troops.

3,000 men, mostly German, French and Italian, many of them
veterans of the First World War and of Fascist concentration
camps, marching with absolute precision and singing revolutionary
songs, paraded across the embattled capital and then moved directly
into the wooded eastern edges of the Casa de Campo. A few hundred
of them were fused in the proportion of roughly one to four among
the militiamen, for whom they set an immediate practical example
in the digging of foxholes, the use of cover and economy of ammunition. The next day the major portion of them bore the brunt of the
Insurgent effort to penetrate the capital via the University City, and
in the following ten days the great majority of them were killed or
wounded.

For ten days, 8–18 November, the battle continued without
pause. Madrid suddenly became the center of the world. From their
hotel rooms near the Plaza de España ace journalists of all countries
followed the fighting in the Casa de Campo and the University
City through binoculars. In the streets they tasted the humor, the
verve and the dignity which were to convert almost all of them into
lifelong champions of the Spanish *pueblo*. The Madrileños returned

95

Buenaventura Durruti, most famous of the anarchist militia chiefs.

in kind the admiration of foreign soldiers and journalists. The cafés were a babel of languages, and Spaniards, hearing an unfamiliar tongue, would come over and embrace the unknown guest. 'Vivan los rusos' served as a toast to cover the twenty-odd nations represented in the International Brigades. And if a Czech or a Pole, knowing not a word of any Romance language, lost his way, a dozen Spaniards would triumphantly accompany him to his hotel or dugout.

On 14 November Buenaventura Durruti, whose column had been holding a sector of the quiet Aragon front, brought his men to Madrid and demanded a dangerous assignment with which to prove the Catalan and libertarian contribution to what had been thus far a Castilian, and Socialist-Communist, defense of the world anti-Fascist capital. His column was dispatched to trenches in the west of the University City where the defenders were trying desperately to prevent the Insurgents from reaching the buildings. They held their ground for several hours against waves of Moorish attackers, but when the enemy got a foothold in the nearby Hall of Philosophy the column panicked and fled, as had so many other militia units once their flank had been turned. Varela's men then reached the Clinical Hospital.

On 16 and 17 November maximum penetration was achieved, and the salient was finally contained by the efforts of the Internationals at the Iron Bridge, the Romero column at Frenchman's Bridge and the Second Brigade of Major Martínez de Aragón (including many Basques) fighting round-the-clock grenade battles from floor to floor of the partially destroyed Hospital. The enraged Durruti demanded new sacrifices of his own men to wipe out their shame. On 21 November he died in mysterious circumstances, close to the front, but apparently shot from behind. His body was returned to Barcelona for a monster funeral whose cortège was led by Luis Companys, President of the Generalitat, García Oliver, anarchist Minister of Justice in the Caballero cabinet, and Vladimir Antonov-Ovseyenko, Stalin's 'Old Bolshevik' consul in Barcelona, who was to be shot in the Soviet purges during 1937.

The Insurgents now combined their last ground advances with a supreme effort to break the city's resistance by bombardment. General Franco had said that he did not intend to destroy Spain's cities, but he had also said that he would never leave Madrid in the hands of the Marxists. On the afternoon of 17 November 2,000 projectiles an hour were landing in the center of the city. Shrapnel shells exploded in wide squares like the Plaza de España. Incendiary shells set the working-class and more modest residential quarters afire. (General Franco had announced that he would not shell the Salamanca district, where the upper middle class, his presumed partisans, lived, and the area was now inundated by people from all over the city seeking shelter from the constant bombardment.) That night German bombers, coming over twelve at a time, and guided

Stricken victims of war.

by the fires, dropped cargo after cargo of both explosives and incendiaries. Madrid had no air-raid shelters and almost no anti-aircraft artillery. The recently arrived Russian fighter planes had greatly reduced the daytime raids, but could not be used effectively at night.

The paternal and earthy General Miaja, who had become, in the words of Julián Zugazagoitia, the brilliant editor of *El Socialista*, 'an accessible myth,' calmed the populace and gave his orders over the radio. He was assisted by three women: Dolores Ibarruri, 'La Pasionaria,' Communist deputy from the Asturias; Margareta Nelkin, a Socialist deputy who had recently joined the Communist Party; and Federica Montseny, an anarchist libertarian and feminist leader. These women upheld popular morale by tirelessly exhorting the soldiers and the largely feminine quartermaster corps, by promising more artillery, more Russian aid, more food supplies, and by denying the many rumors that the Moors had entered this or that district of the city.

It is impossible to know just how much this ordeal of fire and bomb was consciously intended to force a surrender, how much it was the result of sheer frustration, and whether the *Schrecklichkeit* (terror) was recommended principally by Spanish or German officers. Minor panics occurred when shells hit subway stations in which large crowds had taken refuge, and firemen opened several gas mains to prevent possible underground explosions. It is possible

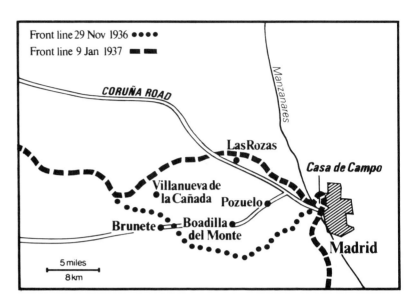

Map of the battle of Coruña road, showing the extent of the Nationalist advance.

that up to 500 people were killed or asphyxiated that night, but in a city of one million inhabitants these deaths produced anger and the will to resist; in the short run at least, they strengthened rather than weakened the morale of the defenders.

On 18 November Italy and Germany announced their diplomatic recognition of the Franco régime, thereby committing themselves fully and publicly to his victory, and lending him a new prestige which was reflected in the increasing use of the term 'Nationalists' rather than 'Insurgents' in the world press. Doubtless they also hoped that their gesture would inspire a final successful effort to storm the capital whose unexpected resistance was threatening to demoralize the attacking army. But the latter simply did not have the numbers, the equipment or the fresh energies to continue the assault on the scale of the 8–18 November period.

Madrid did, however, remain the principal fighting front until late March 1937. From the end of November until mid-January the Nationalists attempted to improve their position west of Madrid, where their communication lines to the Casa de Campo were dangerously thin. On 29 November General Varela attacked north-ward toward Pozuelo and the Coruña highway. German tanks, armed with machine-guns, led the advance, but were forced to retreat in the face of heavier cannon-bearing Russian tanks, and Russian fighter planes proved superior to the early model Stuka dive-bombers which appeared in this battle. Varela renewed the attack for about five days, 16–20 December. Some 12,000 troops (more than twice the number which had assaulted Madrid on 6 November) were thrown into the attack, following the heaviest artillery preparation of the entire war thus far. But Russian tanks and Spanish machine-gunners made the advance too costly, and the battle netted only two small villages, Villanueva de la Cañada and

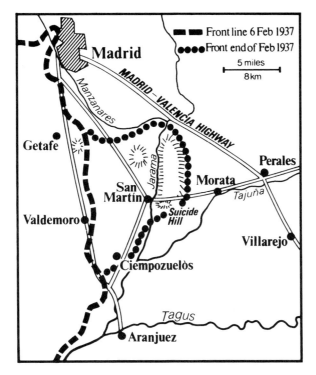

Map of the battle of the river Jarama, illustrating the progress of the Nationalist attempt to encircle Madrid from the south.

Boadilla del Monte. For nine days, 3–11 January, the attack was renewed in the same general sector. The 15,000-man attacking force had overwhelming superiority in firepower, with four batteries (sixteen guns) of 105 mm., four batteries of 155 mm. (the latter capable of knocking out the Russian tanks) and hundreds of 88 mm. guns which were manufactured for anti-aircraft use, but which turned out to be equally serviceable as mobile artillery firing tracer shells at enemy infantry and trenches.

On the Republican side, ammunition was so scarce that General Miaja issued blank cartridges to forward-posted infantry on the theory that if the men heard the sounds of (friendly) firing on their flanks they would hold their lines. Infantry reserves coming up were issued 20 rounds apiece of rifle ammunition in place of the normal 300 rounds. In the course of eight days, General Orgaz secured the Nationalist flank by capturing Las Rozas and cutting the Coruña highway. But the tremendous weight of his armor had not significantly altered the front. The terrain was too rough for rapid, fully coordinated tank maneuvers, and the infantry following the tanks were frequently cut off from communication with their own headquarters. Spanish soldiers, counter-attacking from behind the stone walls of villa gardens and obeying International Brigade officers, had, with machine-gun and bayonet, decimated the Nationalist infantry. Meanwhile, under cover of rolling fog which protected them from enemy artillery, Russian tanks had destroyed strongpoints in Nationalist-held villages, only to lose those villages again when Republican infantry were unable to reoccupy the ground.

The next major effort to encircle Madrid occurred south of the city, in the relatively flat terrain between the Jarama river and the Valencia highway. By 23 January General Orgaz had massed 40,000 troops, of whom about 18,000, spearheaded by Moors, could be thrown into the attack. Each of the five columns had its own anti-tank artillery and two battalions of heavy machine-guns, manned by Germans dressed in Foreign Legion uniforms. Two German tank companies and the Condor Legion bombers were also in readiness. Heavy rains prevented Orgaz from moving until 6 February. The Republican government had known of the Nationalist plans and was simultaneously considering an offensive of its own in the area. Consequently they did not mine the Jarama bridges until after the Nationalist assault began, and the mining was so inexpertly done that when the bridges were blown they settled back into usable if less convenient positions.

The Nationalists quickly occupied the high ground east of the river, and brought the Valencia highway under their artillery fire. Russian tanks slowed their advance at times, but had to retreat as soon as they were brought into range by the German 155 mm. batteries. Condor Legion bombers harassed the Republican infantry, but the latter did not panic, and by 12 February some forty Russian fighter planes had given the Republicans local air superiority. As in the University City during the second week of November, the International Brigades played a critical role. Several hundred Britons held 'Suicide Hill' on the night of 12 February, at a time when the Nationalists might have smashed the Republican lines had they realized that the trenches were empty for several miles south of this gallant British company. But whatever the role of foreign volunteers and equipment, the Battle of the Jarama was also the proud baptism of fire for the new Republican army. Its soldiers had in three months' training learned to handle rifles, machine-guns and mortars as capably as did their Moorish opponents. They had learned also to keep low, move swiftly, not bunch up on the roads when under fire and maintain communication with their officers and their flanking units. General Orgaz had gained ground, but certainly nothing that could be called a strategic victory. He had brought the Valencia highway under fire but had not been able to prevent its use by night. His African troops had been cut to bits, and neither they nor the Foreign Legion would play a leading role as assault troops in future offensives.

The performance of the Republican army made it all the more necessary for General Franco to capture Madrid quickly. He had begun to train a conscript army of his own, but he held the less populous parts of Spain and could not trust a high proportion of his conscripts politically. He was therefore dependent, in his last effort to capture Madrid, on Italian troops, as many as 50,000 of whom

Left: Greetings 1937. Poster issued by the Fifth Regiment, organized by the Communist Party as their contribution to the defense of Madrid.

Right: The clutch of the Italian invader means enslavement. Propaganda by the Madrid defense junta against foreign intervention in the Spanish conflict.

had landed in Spain by the beginning of March. About 5,000 Italians had taken part in the capture of Málaga in February. They had performed creditably, but had not faced any such well-equipped and trained opponents as they would face on the Madrid front.

In early March the Nationalist command concentrated about 50,000 troops near the town of Sigüenza, north-east of Madrid, and some twelve miles by road from the main Saragossa–Madrid highway. Half were Spanish and Moorish troops under General Moscardó, the hero of the siege of the Alcázar; and half were Italians under General Roatta. Their armament included four motorized machine-gun companies, 250 Italian and German light tanks and tractors, 180 heavy artillery, 70 aircraft and several hundred trucks. On 8 March they broke through the Republican lines along a forty-mile front, from the valley of the Henares, north-west of the Saragossa road, to the Tajuna valley south-east of the same highway. But owing to the hills and forests in the area, and to the fact that only the highway was capable of carrying heavy traffic, it was immediately clear to the

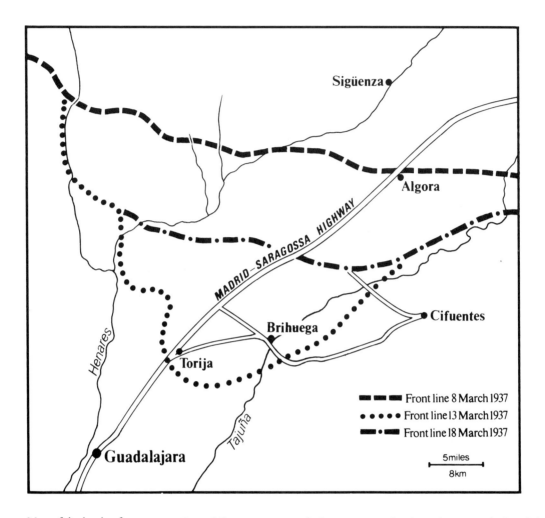

Map of the battle of
Guadalajara, showing the
furthest limits of the
Nationalist advance toward
Madrid and the territory
finally held.

Republican command that a motorized push toward Guadalajara
and Madrid would have to come down the main Saragossa–Madrid
road.

The defense junta transferred its crack troops, the Lister (Communist) and Mera (anarchist) battalions and the International
Brigades, from the Jarama to the vicinity of Torija, where they dug
in rapidly. Spanish and Soviet staff officers established headquarters
in Guadalajara. The next day they began to slow the Italian troops
along the highway north of Torija and in the woods along the road
between Brihuega and Torija. The Nationalists had agreed in
advance that General Orgaz would launch diversionary attacks
along the Jarama front in order to prevent the Republicans from
transferring any large portion of their combat troops. But partly
because his casualties had been so heavy in February, and partly out
of spite toward the boastful Italians, Orgaz did not launch any action
which might have taken the pressure off the forces marching toward
Guadalajara. On 11 and 12 March a snow- and ice-storm halted the

A Cuban volunteer with the International
Brigade appeals to Nationalist troops
to desert to the government side.

long vehicular columns and also prevented Nationalist aircraft from
crossing the Sierra Guadarrama, behind which their airstrips were
located. The Republican planes could fly from closer bases, and were
prepared to risk the icy weather. They bombed the stalled trucks and
tanks almost at will, thereby completely disorganizing the enemy's
transport.

Once the International Brigade leaders had realized that the troops
facing them were uniformed Italian divisions they decided to mount
a propaganda campaign with the hope of causing desertions among
their conscripted compatriots. Pulling loudspeakers up to the lines,
and dropping leaflets from the air, they exhorted the Italian soldiers
not to fire on their brother workers, and guaranteed them immunity
if they would desert to the Republican lines with their arms. On the
other side General Roatta reminded his troops that 'Italy of the Year
XV' (the Fascist era) would be judged by their performance. The
Garibaldis, he told them, were only the brothers of the Marxist
rabble which the Fascist squads had smashed in Italy.

Italian soldiers, 'volunteers' in the fight for Fascism.

For about five days hard local battles continued along the highway, and at several points in the woods along the Brihuega–Torija road. Some dead Garibaldis were found with the leaflets stuffed in their mouths, and here and there a handful of Fascist soldiers deserted. But the available evidence does not suggest that the propaganda played a large role in the outcome of the battle. The Italians had been completely confused when the combination of bad weather and Republican bombing suddenly halted their triumphal march. They had fought hard for several days thereafter but had gradually become demoralized: from the cold, the lack of supplies, the unexpectedly tough resistance and the strange land. They retreated most of the way to Sigüenza but held some of the ground gained in the first successful surprise attack of 8 March. On 18 March their general himself had demanded that they be withdrawn from the front and replaced by Spanish troops. They had lost some 2,000 dead, about 300 prisoners and a mass of material and documents. Spaniards on both sides of the lines snickered at their discomfiture. In café conversation the initials of the expeditionary corps, CTV, were laughingly translated as 'Cuando Te Vas?' ('When are you going home?')

The Italian failure at Guadalajara was the last Nationalist effort to take the city of Madrid. After mid-March 1937, the major battles occurred on other fronts.

Attacked by Italians, Moors
and Germans, fortress
Madrid remains invincible.

Holding aloft the banners of their movement, blue-shirted Falangists mount a ceremonial parade in memory of José Antonio Primo de Rivera, the movement's founder, executed in Alicante in November 1936.

Chapter Six

POLITICAL DEVELOPMENTS:
OCTOBER 1936–MAY 1937

The months which witnessed the series of battles near Madrid were also decisive months in the political evolution of both zones. In the Insurgent area General Francisco Franco had from the first days been the figure of maximum military and political prestige. His African units had spearheaded the offensive toward Madrid. The financiers Juan March and Juan Ventosa, and the wealthy exiled King Alfonso XIII, had between them contributed some $85,000,000 to the Insurgent treasury. Following their example, the entire wealthy upper classes, their friends in the British business community, the German business community in Morocco and the governments of Germany, Italy and Portugal all funneled their material aid to the headquarters of General Franco. By 1 October he had been officially chosen head of the wartime government by his military colleagues and had undertaken personally to refer to himself as 'Head of the State.' On 18 November, ten days after the beginning of the siege of Madrid, his régime had been recognized by Germany and Italy as the sole legitimate government of Spain. In December Great Britain signed a trade agreement with the 'Insurgent Authorities.' In the United States pro-Republican sentiment, the Neutrality Act and isolationist feeling combined to prevent the conclusion of any official trade agreement, but Texaco and Standard Oil, General Motors and Studebaker trucks (items not covered by the neutrality legislation) were sold, largely on credit, to the Insurgent junta.

General Franco had the great advantage of restoring public order rapidly and of exercising strong, visible, consistent authority. He had occupied Spain's major agricultural zones. Food supplies were abundant, and prices were successfully held close to their July 1936 levels during the first months of the war. In his public statements he avoided commitments as to the future form of government, but emphasized the need for central authority and reiterated that the just social reforms of recent years would be retained. He made few references to religion, but enjoyed from the very beginning the

Material help from Germany was crucial to the success of the Nationalist cause. This parade was mounted in honor of the new German ambassador, Eberhard von Stohrer, on his arrival at Salamanca.

strong support of the Church hierarchy in the territory under his control. For several reasons the Church as a whole was wary of committing itself to him publicly. Many of the Insurgent officers had been vociferous anticlericals. The Basque Republicans, who were also ardent Catholics, had opposed the military rising. The Vatican was uncertain whether the Insurgents would eventually win, and it had to consider the sentiments of the Spanish population in both zones. Nevertheless, the General's headquarters in Salamanca were established in the palace of the Archbishop. Personally Franco had not been particularly devout, but the persecution of priests in the 'red' zone had aroused his latent emotions, and the influence of his wife may well have hastened his own evolution toward a new religiosity. In any event, with the passing months he heard Mass

Effigies of Mussolini and Hitler with their lap-dog Franco, on show in an anti-Fascist exhibition held in Valencia.

increasingly frequently and spoke more often of Spain's Catholic tradition and world mission.

For purposes of a long war the General suffered the disadvantage of not having conquered any of his country's major industrial areas. Madrid, Barcelona, Bilbao and Valencia were all in the Republican zone. Not only were their industrial and port facilities unavailable, but their populations constituted a large reservoir of manpower for the incipient Republican army. Even with his smaller manpower reserves he hesitated to resort to conscription of a population which he knew to be largely hostile to his military dictatorship. None of these disadvantages appeared critical until the failure to capture Madrid. By December 1936 German officers were questioning his military competence. Neither *Schrecklichkeit* by artillery and air bombardment, nor infantry assaults, had taken the city which was supposed to have been rapidly occupied in the first week of November. Franco was desperate for both supplies and men. Approximately 25,000 Italian troops had arrived in the peninsula by the end of January 1937, but Mussolini insisted that they be assigned to a front of their own, and not simply be thrown in as replacements in the siege of the capital. On 5 January the General accepted the formation of a ten-man German-Italian staff of 'advisers,' and as of 26 January he had been pushed to concede the possible use of a German-Italian 'general staff' in return for greatly increased armament deliveries.

The failure to achieve quick victory and the pressure of his foreign allies threatened the political stability of his home front. The Insurgents' civilian backing in July 1936 had consisted of the landowners and wealthy businessmen, a considerable proportion of the judiciary and the civil service, and many of the landowning peasants and the Catholic middle class of Navarre and Castile. In pre-war politics these people had supported the conservative Republicans of Alejandro Lerroux, the 'accidentalists' of Gil Robles' CEDA, the Carlists or the Alphonsine monarchists. Neither Lerroux nor Gil Robles had backed the rising until after it had occurred. Both of them, in a situation of civil war, offered their support to the Insurgents, but they were thoroughly distrusted both by the military and by the rightist youth movements. They resided in Lisbon and exercised virtually no influence on their former followers. As for the Alphonsine monarchists, their numbers had always been small, and they disbanded their own party early in 1937.

Thus during the first months of war the only significant civilian political forces in Insurgent territory were the Carlists and the Falange. The Carlists, whose principal strength lay in Navarre, were royalists who supported the claims of a collateral branch of the royal family. They had been dissatisfied with the monarchy since 1833 because, in their opinion, the reigning branch of the Bourbon dynasty had made too many concessions to secular liberalism. They were fanatically Catholic and localist, nourishing their pride on the memory of medieval *fueros*, on prejudices of ethnic superiority to the 'semi-African' population of Mediterranean Spain, on sentiments of moral superiority toward liberals of all sorts, be they monarchists or Republicans, and on utter scorn for the accidentalist position of the CEDA. They were ardent fighters who supplied as many as 30,000 of the Insurgents' finest volunteer troops in the early months, but in politics they were dangerous utopians. The detailed planning of the July rising had been hampered by their insistence, given up only at the last moment, on flying their own flag. In December their leader, Fal Conde, had tried to open a royal officer training academy without the permission of General Franco. The latter had threatened to shoot him, and had in fact exiled him.

As the basis for a mass political party the Falange was much more promising than the Carlist Communion, but was not without its own organizational and ideological problems. Its principal leader, José Antonio Primo de Rivera, son of the late dictator, had been arrested by the Popular Front government in March 1936. He had not been a successful political tactician or impressive theorist. Rather he was a charismatic personality who in many ways symbolized the ideals and the confusions of a whole generation of middle-class youth. As an able but not too serious law student he had considered himself a disciple of the philosopher José Ortega y Gasset and had formed many friendships with both conservative and leftist fellow-students. The gallantry and loyalty which were always characteristic of him

José Antonio Primo de Rivera,
leader of the Falange.

led him publicly to defend his father's reputation, but when in
October 1933 he took part in the founding of the Falange, he defended
neither monarchy nor the recent dictatorship. He said that Spain
needed a revolution, a far more profound revolution, in fact, than
that being attempted by the Republic. He referred to Socialism as
just in its origins and aspirations, and he favored the separation of
Church and state. The trouble with Socialism, for him, was its
dependence on foreign models and its atheism. In his speeches and
writings during the following three years he propounded no specific
program but called for a spirit of sacrifice and national unity. He
paid homage to Mussolini's energy and oratorical prowess without
being particularly impressed with the corporative state. He admired
imperial England, and loved to quote Kipling's 'If,' but he was convinced of the decline of the West. He had many personal friends and
social connections among the monarchists, but he did not think them
capable of leading the regenerated Spain of which he dreamed. He
hoped to draw the industrial workers away from socialism and
anarcho-syndicalism, but neither Falangist membership lists nor the
electoral statistics of 1933–36 indicate any marked success in this
effort. The history of his organization was marked by factional
splits, and these resulted more from personality conflicts than from
clear programmatic differences.

On 13 November 1936 Primo de Rivera was tried in Alicante,
ostensibly for his role in the military rising which had brought civil
war and foreign intervention to Spain. In court he defended himself
by reading from the party organ, *Arriba*, editorials which clearly

differentiated the Falange from both the far Right and the generals. He also noted that the Insurgents had made no effort to free him and had not named him for any future governing post. The evidence concerning his role in the rising reflected the contradictions of his own spirit. He had indeed offered Falangist troops to Mola, but he had condemned the rising in the form in which it actually occurred, probably because he had always dreamed of a true *movimiento nacional* led by the military but based upon a wide popular consensus. The local press lauded the dignity of his behavior in prison and during his trial, but he was condemned to death on 17 November, and the civil governor, disobeying the known directives of the Madrid government, carried out the sentence before the cabinet could review it. The execution angered Largo Caballero for its political stupidity as well as its insubordination. José Antonio left a testament in which he named his ideal government of national union, including a majority of Republicans and moderate Socialists.

Thus during the first days of the siege of Madrid the Falange lost its most attractive and probably its ablest leader. In the Insurgent zone the 'Old Guard' immediately inaugurated the custom of including in its roll call the ritual cry: 'José Antonio, Presente!' Other important leaders were missing also. The transatlantic flyer Ruiz de Alda and José Antonio's brother, Miguel, had been lynched in one of the raids on the Model Prison in Madrid, and Raimundo Fernández Cuesta, later to be exchanged, was still in jail. The Falange in the spring of 1937 had several claimants to leadership, notably the Santander mechanic and party organizer, Manuel Hedilla, and the chief of the party militia, Agustín Aznar, but none of these claimants could muster majority support within the organization.

From General Franco's point of view the Falange represented both an opportunity and a threat. It had expanded rapidly, enrolling many former Marxist and anarchist workers in the populous and left-leaning provinces of Andalusia and Galicia. It had supplied over 100,000 enthusiastic recruits, second in quality only to the much smaller Carlist militia. It made a leftist appeal of its own, calling for agrarian reform and a larger share for labor in the fruits of capitalist industry. At the same time it was anti-Marxist and antiregional. Though some of its rhetoric was anticlerical, its main ideological emphasis was on the Catholic, imperial, centralist tradition of Castile. In all these ways it stood close to the General's own political and religious views. On the other hand many of its local chieftains were crude, undisciplined men, by no means happy to accept a complete military dictatorship and by no means loath to criticize the shortcomings of the Nationalist war effort in the discouraging days after the failure to capture Madrid. On 2 February the Falange attempted to reprint, and rebroadcast, throughout the Nationalist zone, an electoral speech of José Antonio's dating from early February 1936 and excoriating the traditional Spanish Right as well as the Popular Front coalition. Through prompt censorship the

Opposite: Let us direct the energies of the working classes, led astray by Marxism, with the aim of urging their direct participation in the great task of the national state. Nationalist poster, proclaiming unity among all classes, reflects the leftist stamp of Falangist ideology in the early months of the war.

Orientemos el impetu de las clases trabajadoras, descarriadas por el marxismo, en el sentido de exigir su participacion directa en la gran tarea del ESTADO NACIONAL

SERVICIO NACIONAL DE PROPAGANDA - DEPARTAMENTO DE PLASTICA.

authorities prevented the Falange from engaging in this exercise in political agitation. Franco was also well aware that the German ambassador, General Faupel, was giving at least spiritual encouragement to the left wing of the Falange, which involved such prominent, and independent-spirited, personalities as the founder's sister, Pilar Primo de Rivera, the poet and propagandist Dionisio Ridruejo, and Hedilla himself as the would-be Führer.

By early April Franco had decided to fuse the Carlist and miscellaneous Catholic, monarchist and JONS (Juntas de Ofensiva Nacional-Sindicalista) youth groups with the Falange in order to form a single political party under his own absolute control. He intended to name a *secretariado político*, giving majority representation to the less radical fraction of the Falange. Hedilla attempted to head off this development by naming a *junta política* of his own. Personal enmities within the Falange led to a gang fight one night in Salamanca between the adherents of Hedilla and his arch-rival Agustín Aznar. Franco took advantage of the disorders to break Hedilla completely. The left-wing chief was court-martialed and condemned to death. His sentence was commuted, but he nevertheless spent the years 1937–41 in solitary confinement. On 19 April the General announced the unification of the several political parties and militias as the Falange Española Tradicionalista y de las JONS. Thus he forced organizational unity upon the squabbling monarchist and Fascist groups which provided both his most ardent soldiers and his most dangerous political critics. He had demonstrated his cool mastery to both the Falange radicals and the German embassy. He had created the subordinate mass political organization which was to stand him in good stead throughout the war and for at least two decades beyond.

The political problems within the Republican zone were much more severe than those faced by General Franco. Had it not been for massive popular resistance in the main cities, and for the revolt of the sailors which had temporarily prevented the generals from bringing the army of Africa to the mainland, the *pronunciamiento* of 18 July would probably have produced a military-dominated, economically and socially reactionary government, if not a full-dress military dictatorship. Socialist, anarchist and Communist unions and youth organizations were conscious that they, and not the Republican government, had prevented the generals from imposing their will in the first days. A profound and spontaneous social revolution had occurred, albeit in a confused, decentralized, frequently wasteful and violent fashion. No one from the moderate Republicans through to the far Left could deny the popular role in defeating the initial rising, and no one would have denied the necessity and the justice of at least some aspects of the ensuing revolution. But this general spiritual unity did not resolve any of the ideological conflicts within the Popular Front. Nor did it resolve any of the specific military, diplomatic and political problems faced by the Giral and then by the Largo Caballero governments in their efforts to conduct a defensive

war against their own professional army, supported as that army was by Germany, Italy, Portugal and large sectors of the English and American business communities.

Until the end of November everything had depended upon improvisation. Small columns affiliated with student groups or trade unions, and advised by a few dozen professional officers, had defended the Somosierra pass against General Mola in late July and August. In September they had commuted to the Talavera and Toledo fronts. During October workers and students had helped on a part-time, voluntary basis, without much in the way of tools or military know-how, to prepare trenches south and west of Madrid. In November the assault by the invading army had galvanized the moral and physical energies of the city's population, and this, together with the arrival of the first International Brigades, the Russian tanks and fighter planes, had produced the miraculous defense of the capital. As Prime Minister after 4 September, Largo Caballero had brought the Socialist and Communist Parties, and the UGT, into the governing coalition, and on 4 November he had been able to add several very able anarchists to his cabinet. But then his government had fled to Valencia on 6 November, abandoning the capital to what at the time seemed like almost certain enemy occupation.

At the end of November Madrid was being defended and governed by a virtually independent junta, headed by General Miaja, and supported by the Communist Party, the Russian advisers, the Internationals and the overwhelming mass of working people and militiamen. Meanwhile from Valencia the Caballero government began to build a trained army and develop the material resources for a long war. But inevitably there was competition for scarce resources between the Miaja defense junta and the newly organizing central army. Through its complete inability to spare supplies and men the government lost Málaga almost without a struggle in the first week of February. At the Jarama, however, the Republican infantry which had been trained under the supervision of General José Asensio Torrado gave an excellent account of itself, equalling Franco's best troops in its coolness under fire, its ability to dig trenches, use cover and maintain discipline in its movements.

The most important political phenomenon in the Republican zone during these months was the rapid growth of the Communist Party, which had perhaps 50,000 members in July 1936 and which claimed about a million by the middle of 1937. The new membership came largely from the army, the government and the intellectual sectors. The party enrolled military figures such as General Miaja, General Pozas (commanding the central zone south of Madrid) and General Hidalgo de Cisneros (head of the air force). Other important professionals such as Major Vicente Rojo, Miaja's chief of staff, admired and gladly cooperated with the Communist Party and the Soviet staff officers. A number of important Socialists from the Caballero wing of the party, notably Santiago Carrillo, head of the Unified Socialist Youth, joined the Communists; and Julio Álvarez del Vayo, Foreign Minister and a longtime friend of Caballero, cooperated with Communist and Soviet leadership as much as any party member could have been expected to.

Largo Caballero himself had been billed as 'the Spanish Lenin' in the autumn of 1936. But the attitude of the Communists toward him was largely condescending and manipulatory. They admired his proletarian origins, his trade union work and his personal integrity. They recognized his immense importance as a symbolic and unifying figure for the Popular Front in the dark days before the successful defense of Madrid. They expected his younger pro-Communist friends to 'guide' him as Prime Minister. But Largo Caballero was a very proud man, and very punctilious concerning his authority. He resented the constant advice of the Soviet ambassador, Marcel Rosenberg, and was intensely jealous of Miaja. He was not to be disturbed at night, would sign papers only at certain hours, demanded receipts and accounts as if he were running a country general store in time of peace.

As a result also of personal jealousy he failed to make full use of the most talented and energetic civilian leader in the Republican zone, Indalecio Prieto. More significantly he came into conflict with the

LAS OCHO CONDICIONES DEL PARTIDO COMUNISTA PARA GANAR LA GUERRA

Communists over fundamental political ethics. The Party was determined physically to purge the POUM, accused of being 'Trotskyite,' and also to liquidate assorted militant anarchists and Left-Socialists. Theoretically the Communists were opposed to terrorism and assassination, but in fact they resorted to such methods, and they expected the government silently to accept if not to condone their actions. At the same time they wished to woo the middle class at home and the democratic powers abroad. Hence they followed a policy of suppressing revolution by any means available and they proclaimed that the Civil War was being fought solely to defend liberal capitalist democracy. Largo Caballero, on the other hand, was determined both to rebuild the constitutional authority of the state and to defend the revolutionary gains and the political liberties of the Spanish people. Thus he favored the efforts of lawyers such as Rafael Supervia to restore defendants' rights in political trials, and he enthusiastically supported the prison reform efforts of his Basque Minister without Portfolio, Manuel de Irujo. Likewise he refused categorically to suppress the newspapers and the party organizations of the non-Stalinist Left. Though he did call for the

Part of a Spanish Communist Party pamphlet insisting on discipline, conscription and increased production to win the war.

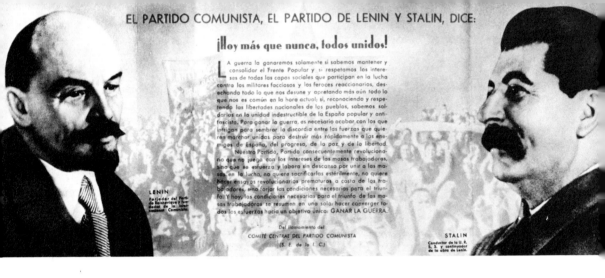

integration of the remaining militia units into the Republican army, he did not move as decisively in this area as both the Communists and the professional officers wished.

Gradually, between November 1936 and May 1937, two coalitions formed within the Republican zone. Against the Prime Minister stood many of the middle-class republicans, the moderate Socialists, and the Communists, in an alliance based upon the all-out defense of Madrid, the restraint of proletarian revolution, the need for strongly centralized government and the growing conviction that Largo Caballero did not have the energy and ability to remain as wartime Premier. On the other side stood the bulk of the UGT and CNT membership, united in fear of the Communists and in defense of the regional collectivist authorities established in the first days of the war. Against the Communist call for cooperation with the bourgeoisie, they insisted that the war could not be won unless the proletarian revolution were won simultaneously.

Late in March, after the Battle of Guadalajara, the subterranean political struggle came into the open in Madrid. The CNT prison delegate, Melchor Rodríguez, published precise information concerning torture in unofficial Communist prisons, the victims of which were often released prisoners who had been kidnapped by the Communists. Rodríguez was an autodidact, a philosophical anarchist, absolutely fearless personally, and absolutely opposed to terrorism. Prisoners of all political affiliations had benefited from his humanity, and the scandal was enormous when he not only cited the practices but named as responsible the Communist councilor of public order, José Cazorla. The incident enabled the Prime Minister simultaneously to strike a blow at terrorism and to re-establish the authority of the Valencia government in Madrid. The defense junta accepted Cazorla's resignation, and on 23 April the junta itself was dissolved.

Back in November the government, imitating the example of the Russian Revolution of 1917, had created a corps of political com-

LA VOZ DEL PARTIDO COMUNISTA

TODO el pueblo español, todo lo que hay de sano y progresi-
en nuestro país, está luchando para defenderse de una ag
sión cobardemente perpetrada a mansalva por españoles t
dores a su patria y contra las fuerzas invasoras del fascismo a
mán, italiano y portugués, que sueñan con convertir a España
un pueblo de esclavos.

Luchamos encarnizadamente y con toda la fuerza que dar
derecho y la razón para aniquilar a nuestros enemigos, po
nuestra lucha es una lucha por la democracia, la paz y la libert
y nuestro triunfo, el triunfo del pueblo español, servirá para
mentar la paz y no para perturbarla, desencadenando la guer
como es el negro designio de los fascistas españoles y extranjer

Que todo esto sirva, en fin, para fortalecer todavía más
unión entre todos. ¡Y desgraciado de aquel que, por impacien
o por irresponsabilidad, entorpezca esta unión y retrase la ho
de la victoria!

Nuestro Partido, el Partido Comunista, que por su organiz
ción, cada día más pujante, es fiel intérprete de la voluntad po
lar, declara una vez más que, aun estimando que su fuerza re
no se halla suficientemente representada en la dirección oficial
país, ocupará, como siempre, sin vacilaciones ni regateos, un pue
de vanguardia en la resolución de todos los problemas que plant
la necesidad de ganar la guerra. Y está seguro de que los m
cianos y las fuerzas leales de mar, tierra y aire, de que todos
trabajadores y todos los hombres libres y progresivos de Espa
apretarán todavía más sus filas en torno a él, que ha sido el f
jador del Frente Popular, eje de la República democrática, y
que todos juntos, cordialmente compenetrados y férreamente u
dos, con el arrojo y la abnegación de que da pruebas nues
pueblo, GANAREMOS LA GUERRA.

Del llamamiento del
COMITÉ CENTRAL DEL PARTIDO COMUNISTA
(S. E. de la I. C.)

PARTIDO COMUNISTA señala **EL CAMINO DE LA VICTORIA**

missars whose duty was to educate the militia to the needs of military discipline and centralized authority, and to monitor the politics of potentially 'unreliable' professional officers. Caballero had appointed his then trusted collaborator Julio Alvarez del Vayo to head the commissariat. As a fellow-traveler Del Vayo had appointed dozens of Communist commissars without the knowledge of the Prime Minister. Caballero now proposed to destroy this particular source of Communist power. On 17 April he published a decree stating that all future nominations would be made directly by the Prime Minister, and that all current commissars must have their appointments validated by 15 May. A bitter press debate followed. *Adelante*, the Caballero organ, accused the commissars of political pressure, favoritism and occasional assassination. *Frente Rojo*, the Communist organ, saw the decree as the work of 'Fascist elements' and urged the commissars to stick to their posts. *El Socialista*, organ of the Prieto wing, published the names of Socialist Party militants who had been tortured in private Communist prisons in Murcia.

Continuing tensions within the Catalan Left, and government efforts to regain control of the Catalan-French frontier, led to a brief civil war within the civil war. On 17 April the *carabineros*, acting on the authority of the Finance Minister, Juan Negrín, began to reoccupy frontier posts which had been patrolled by the anarchists since 18 July the previous year. At least eight anarchists were killed in clashes with the *carabineros*. A prominent UGT official, Roldán Cortado, was murdered, probably by CNT elements, and his funeral in Barcelona was the occasion of a massive demonstration against the anarchists. When Caballero also announced his intention to militarize the remaining worker militias of Catalonia, the POUM and the anarchist press sounded the alarm. Militarization, for them, was simply a euphemism for disarmament and repression of the class-conscious revolutionary workers. Tension was such that the Generalitat canceled the scheduled May-Day celebration, fearing pitched battles between the police and the anti-Stalinist Left. Among

The other side of the pamphlet shown on page 117. The portraits are of Lenin, Stalin, José Díaz (General Secretary of the Party) and Dolores Ibarruri, 'La Pasionaria.'

the public services still controlled at this time by the anarchists was the telephone company, administration of which enabled them to listen in on government conversations with Valencia or Madrid, and to monitor all foreign calls originating from or directed to Barcelona and Valencia. On 3 May Rodríguez Salas, Councilor for Public Order in the Generalitat and a member of the PSUC, intended, peaceably he hoped, but by force if necessary, to take control of the central Barcelona telephone exchange. When he arrived with a company of Assault Guards he was met by fire from within the building.

This skirmish led to three days of sporadic fighting all over the city. POUM and anarchist troops assembled at Barbastro and prepared to march to Barcelona in order to defend their brothers from the 'counter-revolutionary' *putsch*. Luis Companys, the anarchist ministers in the Caballero government and *Solidaridad Obrera* (the anarchist paper) all appealed for an immediate cease-fire. The revolutionaries were deeply divided as to tactics. All of them instinctively hated the Assault Guards, and all of them demanded the removal of the principal PSUC councilors. The CNT and the POUM officially ordered their followers only to 'defend' themselves, but this settled nothing, since the whole question was whether the government or the separate political parties were going to control the public services of Catalonia. Small but vehement anarchist groups, the Libertarian Youth and the Friends of Durruti, encouraged armed resistance in the name of the revolutionary conquests which alone made worthwhile the maintenance of the Popular Front.

On 5 May Companys obtained a fragile truce, on the basis of which the PSUC councilors were to retire from the regional government, and the question of the telephone company was left to future negotiation. That very night, however, Antonio Sesé, a UGT official who was about to enter the reorganized cabinet, was murdered. In any event, the Valencia authorities were in no mood to temporize further with the Catalan Left. On 6 May several thousand Assault Guards arrived in the city, and the Republican navy demonstrated in the port. Caballero named General Sebastián Pozas, who had recently become a Communist, to command the army of Aragon. The Left militia was disarmed, and military discipline was established on the Aragon front. The Prime Minister pledged himself against political reprisals, but in the following few days a dozen anti-Communist Left leaders were the victims of assassinations motivated in part by revenge for the UGT deaths of the recent past, in part by Communist determination to liquidate physically the anti-Stalinist leadership in Barcelona.

In Valencia the Communist ministers insisted that Largo remove the Minister of the Interior, Angel Galarza, for failure to uncover the 'Trotskyite plot' in Barcelona, and demanded the suppression of *La Batalla*, the POUM organ, as having incited rebellion. The Prime Minister saw no evidence to justify either demand. On 13 May, at a cabinet meeting, the ministers demanded the suppression of the POUM; when Caballero refused to take up the question, they walked out, thereby precipitating a cabinet crisis.

The many-faceted struggle between the Prime Minister and his enemies now came to a head. The Communists attacked him because of his threat to their control of the commissars and because of their pathological hatred of the POUM. But both Republicans and anarchists had on several occasions opposed his military judgment, and the anti-Communist Left would hardly rise to his defense after the Barcelona events. The moderate Socialists, in turn, were by no means averse to the political (as against the physical) liquidation of the Trotskyites, anarchists and 'infantile leftists' of the Caballero wing.

Still, in precipitating the cabinet crisis of 13 May, the Communists did not wish to appear responsible for the overthrow of Spain's first working-class Prime Minister. During the presidential consultations for the formation of a new government, they told Azaña that they would continue to collaborate with him providing he relinquished the war portfolio, which office should be filled by Prieto. But Caballero's pride, his view of his own responsibility in the creation of the new army and his old rivalry with Prieto would not permit him to accept this solution, and he resigned, as his enemies hoped he would.

The new Prime Minister, Dr Juan Negrín, was an internationally known physiologist who had been a leading professor and part-time administrator in the University of Madrid. He was a Socialist, and had served as Minister of Finance in the Caballero government. He brought great energy and executive ability to his new office, was on excellent personal terms with the Republican and parliamentary Socialist leaders, with the professional officers, with the Communists, the Russians and the foreign press. His government was administratively more efficient than Caballero's, and was fully supported by the Communists and the army, but it was passively accepted rather than truly supported among the regionalists and the non-Communist Left. Thus, in contrast with the increasing unity achieved during the spring of 1937 in the Nationalist zone, Republican Spain remained sorely divided. Just as the appointment of Largo Caballero had symbolized the unity of the Popular Front, so his forced resignation indicated the growing disunity within Republican Spain.

Juan Negrín and Manuel Azaña, by mid-1937 the Republic's chief political leaders.

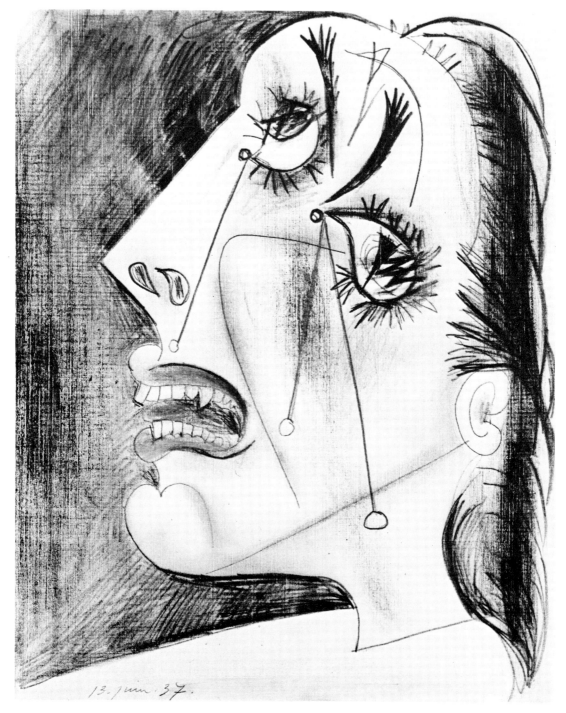

Study by Picasso for his famous painting commemorating the attack on Guernica.

Chapter Seven

A YEAR OF WAR:
APRIL 1937 – APRIL 1938

After the battles of the Jarama and Guadalajara General Franco turned his attention to the northern front. In early 1937 there were several reasons why it would seem relatively easy, and highly desirable, to conquer this area. The zone comprising the Basque provinces, Santander and most of Asturias was geographically isolated from the rest of Republican Spain. The Basque Nationalists were devoutly Catholic, and in the course of centuries, first of the wool trade and more recently of the steel and shipping industries, they had looked to England or France for models of education, economic organization and political behavior. They were fighting the Burgos junta because they opposed military dictatorship and blood purges and because the Republic had granted them their long-sought Statute of Autonomy. But their whole outlook was much more conservative than that of the Asturian miners, and they were not likely to establish relations of genuine cooperation with revolutionary Socialists and anarchists anywhere. The Burgos authorities were therefore confident that they would not face desperate resistance from the Basques. At the same time, having begun the war without an industrial base, they were anxious to acquire the iron ore, the steel mills, the shipyards and port facilities of Bilbao. They realized also that the reluctance of British capitalist circles and of the Vatican to give all-out backing to their movement was due to the fact that the Basque Nationalists had sided with the Republic.

After the Insurgent capture of Irún on 4 September 1936, the northern front had been quiet. The Basques had established lightly held defense lines east of Elgoibar and along the hilltops north of Vitoria. They were constructing a so-called 'Iron Ring' a few miles from the perimeter of their capital city. They had about 30,000 to 40,000 trained militia of their own and an undetermined number of men belonging to the various parties of the Popular Front. They possessed perhaps forty field-guns, caliber 75 mm. and 155 mm., and lots of 81 mm. mortars. In October a single Russian ship had arrived at Bilbao bringing twelve aircraft and twenty-five armored cars which mounted 47 mm. cannon and heavy machine-guns. On the other side, by the end of March, General Mola had collected 50,000 well-equipped Navarrese, Moroccan and Italian troops. His German and Italian planes had full command of the air while bombing Basque entrenchments and the Bilbao port area during the first months of the year. He had ample trucks and petroleum, telephone and radio teams, which were operated independently (and very efficiently) by the Germans, and the German 88 mm. anti-aircraft guns, whose primary function was not necessary in the absence of a Basque air force but which did excellent service as mobile artillery. The offensive was launched on 31 March, and advanced steadily, but with disappointing slowness. Much of the country was wooded and hilly, without real motor roads. The Basques were economical of men and supplies, but had built effective tank traps and barbed-wire entanglements. They retreated in good order, slowly, and they exacted a high price in disabled vehicles and in overly audacious attacking infantry.

One action of the spring campaign caused an immediate international scandal, and, through being immortalized in a mural by Pablo Picasso, became probably the most famous single incident in the entire war: the bombing of Guernica. Guernica was a small market town, without military defenses or objectives other than a bridge over the river Mundaca which, if destroyed, would hamper the retreat of the Basque army westward toward Bilbao. It was also the ancient capital of the Basque nation. The Condor Legion fliers, who had already bombed Durango, Eibar and several smaller villages probably had no idea of the symbolic importance of Guernica. Nationalist officers, on the other hand, would have known it as the spiritual capital of the Basque people and some of them were undoubtedly motivated by the desire to humiliate and terrorize the Basques precisely because the latter were felt to be 'traitors' to the cause of Nationalist, Catholic Spain. From the point of view of Hermann Goering and the Condor officials, as revealed in 1946 at the Nuremberg war crimes trials, Guernica offered excellent laboratory conditions for the testing of both explosive and incendiary bombing methods.

Monday, 26 April, was a market day. The weather was clear, and during the afternoon the local hospital was receiving the wounded from air raids that morning on nearby villages. The air attack, as described by townspeople who survived it, took place in three stages: explosive bombs and packets of hand-grenades dropped by Junker Ju-52 planes; machine-gunning of those running in the streets and along roads, performed by Heinkel He-111 fighter planes; drenching of the area with incendiary bombs. The repeated strikes occurred between 4:50 and 7:30 p.m., with visibility excellent until the sky was obscured by smoke. The bridge over the Mundaca was not hit. At least 200 people were killed and many more wounded.

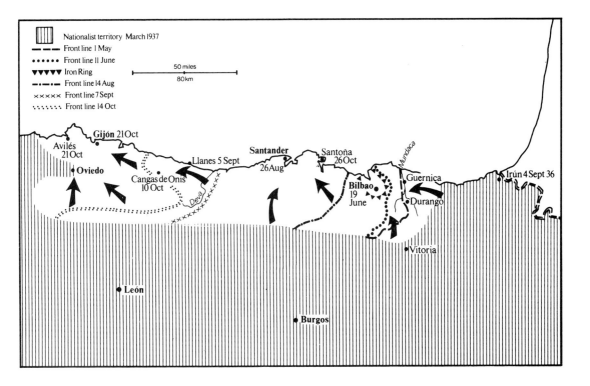

Map showing the course of the Nationalist advances on the northern front.

Accounts the following day in the French press led to an international outcry. Catholic intellectuals like Jacques Maritain and François Mauriac excoriated the Nationalists, and many French Catholics who opposed the Popular Front quickly identified themselves with the unarmed Basque peasants. Men of all political viewpoints who were capable of elementary foresight could anticipate what might happen in the form of aerial bombing of crowded cities if general war should again break out in Europe. Much of the population of Navarre, and some of Mola's best troops, were also outraged. General Franco in all likelihood had not known that the raid would take place. Hitler demanded that the Burgos authorities issue a statement clearing Germany of all responsibility, and on 29 April the Nationalist press announced that the city had been burned by retreating 'reds,' a desperate myth which might have had some degree of credibility because the anarchists had indeed burned portions of Irún when abandoning that city the previous September.

Several French and British correspondents made detailed investigations of their own within a few days, and the original story of the bombing had the unchallengeable authority of Canon Albert Onaindía, an eyewitness who was known and fully trusted by many of the highest officials in the Spanish Church. Until thirty years later, however, it remained a crime in Spain to say that Guernica had been bombed. Only in 1967 was a young Navarrese priest acquitted in Madrid after being indicted for the 'calumny' of writing that

The raid on Guernica. *Right:* Condor Legion pilots plan their attack before take-off. *Below:* one of the Legion's Heinkel He-III fighters on a bombing mission. *Opposite:* the ruins of the town, once the proud capital of the Basque nation, and a victim, made homeless by the bombing.

Guernica had been destroyed by the Nationalist air force. Such was the sensitivity of the Franco government concerning an incident which must seem almost banal after the deeds of the German, British and American air forces in the years since 1937.★

During May the Nationalists continued their slow, methodical advance westward and north toward Bilbao, and during the first days of June the Condor planes and artillery bombarded the 'Iron Ring' and forced the abandonment of many trenches and pill-boxes

★ The truth about Guernica has been succinctly summarized by Eléna de la Souchère, in an article entitled 'Guernica,' *Figaro Littéraire, number 1131, 18 December, 1967*. Treatment of the incident by the world has been studied in immense depth and detail in Herbert R. Southworth, *Gernika! Gernika!* (Paris: Ruedo Ibérico, 1973).

without a fight. Over and above the fact that the plans had earlier been betrayed by one of the engineers who had drawn them up, the 'Iron Ring' showed the same general weaknesses as did most Republican fortifications. Its trenches formed a thin perimeter in the hills outside the city, and in most areas there were only two lines, 200 to 300 yards apart. They stood on the crests, with the generally uncamouflaged concrete visible to the enemy, without positions in depth on the counterslope and without protection on the flanks. Both political and military commentators at the time suspected treason in the entire planning of the defense of Bilbao, but the errors in these fortifications – as in those south of Madrid in October 1936 – could just as well have arisen from the military inexperience of those who designed them. In any case it is difficult to believe that Basque

Nationalist troops occupy Bilbao, which fell to General Dávila's forces without a battle on 19 June 1937.

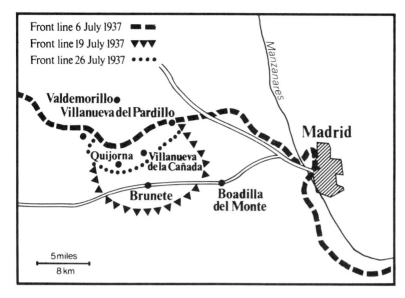

Map showing the Republican offensive launched toward Brunete in an attempt to turn the left flank of the army besieging Madrid.

engineers purposely planned a trench system which would be un-tenable for their sons and brothers.

General Mola was killed in an airplane accident on 3 June, but his death did not interrupt the advance. The defense ring was pierced on 12 June. For a week thereafter Basque, Asturian and Santander militia units retreated westward while the Basque police guarded factories against sabotage, and prisons against popular violence. Motor boats and fishing launches slipped away, some with refugees headed for Saint-Jean-de-Luz in France, others with men intending to carry on the struggle further west. Altogether perhaps 200,000 persons temporarily fled the city. On the 19th General Dávila's army entered Bilbao without opposition and began immediately to distribute food to the thousands of women lining the streets.

Meanwhile the new Republican government of Juan Negrín was eager to take the offensive, in order to relieve the pressure on the northern front and in order to prove that the Republican army was capable of more than defensive actions. The best equipment, the most experienced troops and the most capable general staff (along with its Russian advisers) were present at Madrid. Psychologically too, Madrid was still, for Spaniards on both sides, the main front. The village of Brunete, held by the Nationalists, was an important road junction less than 15 miles west of the capital. In this area the thinly held lines faced each other from east to west. If the Republicans could drive south, to and beyond Brunete, they would be able to envelop the besieging army and lift the siege of Madrid. Near the village of Valdemorillo they concentrated 50,000 men, including the battle-hardened divisions of Lister (Communist), 'El Campesino'

129

(anarchist turned Communist) and three of the International Brigades (foreign in leadership but mostly Spanish in personnel). They had a good supply of Verdun-vintage machine-guns and grenades, and approximately 80 pieces of Vickers-Armstrong artillery manufactured for the Tsarist army in 1916. They were supported by about 100 Russian tanks, and by perhaps 100 Russian planes, in both cases manned by Spanish crews and pilots.

On 6 July the attack achieved a surprise breakthrough, advancing some five miles to surround and then storm Brunete. But even in the first two to three days of initiative the Republican troops lost invaluable time reducing minor points of resistance instead of maintaining their forward momentum. Within three days General Varela was able to move up 30,000 reinforcements, and by the end of the sixth day he had 50,000 new troops, plus the bulk of the Italian and German air forces hastily transferred from the northern front. On flat, sunbaked ground, at temperatures of over 100 degrees in the shade, the two armies fought the most sanguinary battle of the war thus far. Republicans fighting to hold the ground captured in the first few days and Nationalists rushing to counterattack were equally prodigal of men. Both armies mistakenly rained shells on their own forward lines; communications failures and cowardice led to near-mutiny and battlefield executions in several Republican units. Overhead as many as 200 planes appeared on 10 and 11 July while the Republicans tried to maintain their initial air superiority. Until 19 July they held the bulge they had created in taking Brunete, but by this time the weight of Nationalist artillery and air power was overwhelming and all Republican reserves had been committed.

From 19 to 26 July the attackers retreated almost to their starting-point. German pilots exulted in their unchallenged command of the air and marveled at the tenacity of the defenders who could be dislodged from their trenches only by repeated direct hits. Hundreds who could have saved their lives by earlier retreat died running under the machine-gun fire of Heinkels and Messerschmitts. In villages near the front young girls from convent schools, who had been sheltered from all knowledge of human biology, silently treated the delirious, blaspheming wounded. Penicillin had not yet been discovered, and young doctors learned experimentally that gangrene would not set in so frequently after amputations if the wounds were left open. On both sides buses went out each night to bring in the casualties who could not be reached under shellfire during the day. In Madrid, a lightly wounded Russian colonel, seeing the offensive broken, committed suicide.

The Battle of Brunete retarded by only a few weeks the progress of the Nationalist campaign in the north. Theoretically the Republicans had established a unified command under General Gamir Ulibarri, but the Basques were at sword-point with the Asturian and Santander leftist militia. The former wished always to evacuate intact whatever territories they could not hold, while the

A party of Franco's troops passing buildings wrecked during the closing stages of the operations in Santander, taken by Nationalist forces on 26 August 1937.

latter favored a scorched-earth policy. After the fall of Bilbao the Nationalist blockade of the northern coast was almost complete, and the Negrín government was unable to spare enough ships or planes to deliver supplies at Santander and Gijón. For the Italians and the Navarrese the Santander campaign was a military romp. Their main problems were to maneuver their trucks on the narrow, winding roads; to read poor maps under cloudy skies; and to keep their planes from hitting mountainsides.

At the approach of the conquering army to Santander in late August, the Basque authorities at the port of Santoña tried to arrange a separate peace with the Italian forces of General Bastico. The Italians had on several occasions been horrified by the reprisal policies of their Spanish allies, and they were of course flattered to be treated as the supreme authorities on the north coast. The Basques proposed to surrender their arms to the Italians, to maintain public order and to prevent the destruction of property and the killing of hostages. In return General Bastico undertook to guarantee the lives of the Basque soldiers, to authorize the emigration of their officials and to use his influence to protect the Basque population against political persecution. Nationalist officers, hearing of the move, dispatched troops immediately and arrived in Santoña just as the first boatloads of Basques were preparing to weigh anchor. They were all arrested, and the situation of the Basque people generally was perhaps worsened by this attempt to avoid surrendering to the Spanish Nationalist army. Such a separate surrender would also have left the other elements of the Popular Front to the tender mercies of Burgos. The incident greatly embittered relations within the Republican camp.

On 26 August the victors paraded through Santander, complete with giant portraits of Mussolini, and the Italian press celebrated its revenge for the humiliation of Guadalajara. On 21 October, with the fall of Gijón and Avilés, the northern war was over. The docks and mills had already been repaired in Bilbao, and iron ore was being exported after only about a month's interruption. Roads, railroads and docks were being rebuilt by prisoners of war. The most ardent fighters had swelled the ranks of the guerrilla bands in the Cantabrican mountains, but the majority of the population, undernourished and morally depressed, passively accepted the new régime. The Navarrese and Italian divisions were ready for transfer to another front.

On 24 August the Republicans launched a limited offensive in Aragon against the thinly defended towns of Quinto and Belchite. They achieved local success, at great cost, and this action did not constitute a significant threat to the plans of General Franco. It was, however, politically important. The Aragon front had been quiet since early autumn 1936, in part because the fighting had centered around Madrid, in part because these lines, and their rural hinterland, were controlled by the anarchists and the anti-Stalinist POUM. Some 300,000 peasants had formed agricultural collectives here under the general governance of the anarchist-dominated Consejo de Aragon, whose authority had been recognized by the Caballero government. Testimonials concerning the long-run prospects of these collectives vary greatly, but they agree on the fact that, spurred by enthusiastic popular participation and by the new-found sense of dignity among relatively poor and uneducated peasants, there had been a considerable increase in agricultural harvests thus far in 1937. From the government point of view, however, this was politically an unreliable area and one which was not delivering its share of produce and soldiers to the Republican army. In preparation for the Quinto-Belchite operation the Negrín government dissolved the Consejo and placed the area under its direct control. At the same time, recognizing popular sentiment, they did not dissolve the collectives. This was to be performed in March 1938 by the Nationalists when they overran the entire province.*

* Hugh Thomas, 'Anarchist Agrarian Collectives in the Spanish Civil War,' in Raymond Carr (ed.), *The Republic and the Civil War in Spain* (London, Macmillan, 1971), pp. 239–56; G. Jackson, 'The Origins of Spanish Anarchism,' in *The Southwestern Social Science Quarterly* (Sept. 1955), pp. 135–47; G. Jackson, 'The Living Experience of the Spanish Civil War Collectives,' in *Newsletter of the Society for Spanish and Portuguese Historical Studies* (April 1970), pp. 13–20.

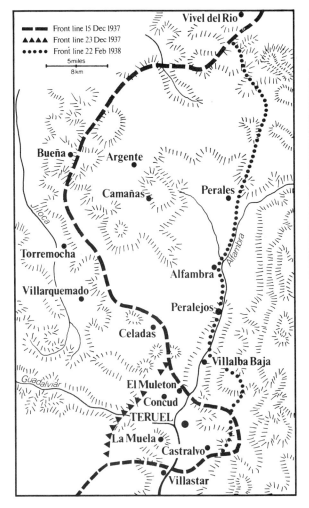

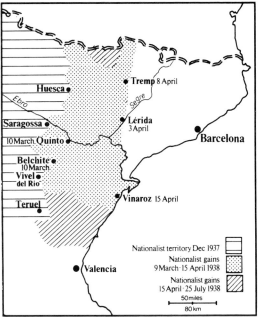

Map of the battle of Teruel illustrating the fluctuations of the battle-lines. The sketch on the right shows the Nationalist army's rapid sweep to the French border and the Mediterranean after its success at Teruel.

In November and December 1937 the Nationalists were gathering men and supplies for a new offensive against Madrid, the capture of which would presumably end the war. The Republican government and army retained their will to battle, but they had consumed their best armament at Brunete. The Russians had lost several freighters sunk in the Mediterranean, and they were becoming increasingly concerned with the threat of Japanese military action along their Far Eastern frontiers. At least by September they had notified Valencia that the latter would have to provide their own ships for future deliveries of Russian *matériel*.

Once more the Republic turned to the preventive offensive as its only means to avoid slow but sure defeat. The Minister of Defense, Indalecio Prieto, and his finest Spanish staff officers, Colonels Hernández Sarabia and Vicente Rojo, chose Teruel as the site of their operation. Located on high rocky bluffs above the junction of the rivers Alfambra and Guadalaviar, the city was known to be lightly held, and it constituted a salient approximately two-thirds surrounded by long-existing Republican lines. For this offensive they gathered 90,000 to 100,000 troops (practically all of them Spanish); the First World War Russian and European field-guns which they had been able to transport from Marseilles or buy from contrabandists; all the rifle and machine-gun ammunition, the grenades, fuses, shells and trucks remodeled as armored-cars which had been produced in 1937 by Catalan factories. They knew of Franco's decision to storm Madrid on 18 December. They planned their attack for a week earlier, then postponed it by four days because of a locomotive strike in Barcelona.

At 7 o'clock on the bitter cold, windy morning of 15 December, 40,000 troops opened the assault without artillery preparation. The Nationalists, who had only about 18,000 troops in and near Teruel, were taken completely by surprise. In conditions of light snow the advance was rapid during the first two days, and the XXII Army Corps coming down from the north made a junction with the XVIII Corps from the south, thereby isolating the city from the main Nationalist lines a few miles to the west. A blizzard on the 17th slowed operations, but the next day the Republicans captured the heights of La Muela which dominated Teruel from the south. Poor weather conditions stalled trucks and grounded planes, a factor which in the circumstances was relatively favourable to the Republicans, whose best weapon was their large mass of well-trained, combative infantry. On 22 December they occupied part of the city, but in the following week were not able to make new gains either within the town or against the Nationalist lines.

In immediate response to the Republican offensive General Franco had sent massive reinforcements. Counter-attacking on 29 December, troops under General Varela recaptured La Muela within twenty-four hours. On New Year's Eve, a night of blinding snow, the Republican troops in the city panicked, and for about four hours the Varela units could have walked in, had they known what was happening in the enemy camp. The next day, with discipline re-established, the Republicans began a street-by-street, building-by-building, struggle against Colonel d'Harcourt's garrison of about 2,500 men. Tanks and armoured cars would blast buildings which had been converted into strongpoints. Machine-gunners rushed to the roofs, and would then hold enemy windows under fire while dynamiters advanced slowly up the street. By 5 January the defending garrison was isolated in the cellar of one of the main buildings, cut off from water and encumbered by several hundred civilian refugees, including the bishop of Teruel and the chairman of the local Red Cross. Emerging under a white flag, the latter asked permission to evacuate the wounded from the Assumption Hospital, which had been isolated, but not touched, by the entering troops. Prieto seized the opportunity to humanize the war on one of the few occasions when the Republicans held the upper hand. He guaranteed the hospital evacuation and also promised security against reprisal for all people of non-military age who had taken refuge with the garrison. On 7 January, after the old, the women and the children had left the cellar, the famished garrison demanded of their leader that he surrender their hopeless position. Colonel d'Harcourt, taken to Valencia as a prisoner, was insulted by the Nationalist press for his 'cowardice,' and a year later was assassinated by 'guards' during the last retreat of the defeated Republican army in the Pyrenees.

For another two weeks the occupants were troubled by snipers. Meanwhile the Nationalist command was gathering some 80,000 to 90,000 fresh troops, several hundred German and Italian planes and abundant Italian field-guns. Snow and subzero temperatures postponed the counteroffensive until the beginning of a considerable thaw on 15 January. The principal Nationalist aim was to push back the enemy lines north-west of the city and, through an enveloping movement, force its evacuation. Exercising complete domination of the air, and possessing substantial artillery superiority, Nationalist troops captured the high ground around Celadas and Muleton between 17 and 19 January. The Republicans counterattacked in the hills north of Celadas on 27–29 January, and then the Nationalists fought their way into the town of Alfambra on 5–7 February, thereby threatening to outflank the city from the north. Driving rains again delayed operations in the middle of the month, but by 18 February the armies of General Aranda to the north and of General Varela to the south were ready to encircle the city. In three days they forced a general retreat eastward. On 22 February the last soldiers under the command of 'El Campesino' fought their way out of the city, and the defeated army left behind the carcasses of several hundred trucks, forty tanks, about eighty pieces of artillery and hundreds of machine-guns.

The able Nationalist military historian, Luis María de Lojendio, wrote that the victors took 17,000 prisoners, whose services they used to bury 9,763 corpses, and that in all the Republicans lost 14,000 dead and 20,000 wounded. This would mean a total of 51,000 casualties, or more than half the enemy forces involved from 15 December to 22 February. By way of contrast, General Rojo, the Republican chief of staff, later wrote that the Republic had suffered 6,000 battle deaths at Teruel. However, casualties must have been very high, because of the large numbers involved (close to 100,000 for each side), because of the dense concentration of artillery in a small area, because the snow outlined moving objects even at night, because the lines swayed back and forth with the numerous local attacks, and because buildings in the city were contested floor by floor. It is thus quite possible that the Republican army lost as many as 14,000 men killed. In any event it was unable to offer serious resistance to further Nationalist attacks during the ensuing two months.

The battle of Teruel. *Above:* Colonels Vicente Rojo and Hernández Sarabia, commanders of the government forces seen, *below,* in the city after its fall on 7 January 1938.

Right: the civilian population evacuating Teruel after its capture. *Below:* Nationalist reinforcements trudge through the snow during the counterattack which by 22 February had compelled the government troops to abandon their positions.

At both Brunete and Teruel the intelligence specialists of all the European armies were judging the performance and the tactics of the Russian, Italian and German tanks. The low-silhouetted, heavily armored Russian vehicles moved forward accompanied by infantry, but the latter were rarely able to follow closely enough for co-ordinated action. The tank crews, cooped up with hot, clanking machinery, and usually having little previous experience as drivers, became confused by poor visibility. Their machines were easily isolated and often captured intact. General von Thoma, in charge of the Condor Legion tanks, claimed in 1938 to have added some sixty Russian machines to his forces, most of them captured by Moors who had been paid 500 pesetas per vehicle. The Germans insisted that their tanks, which were somewhat lighter and faster than the Soviet models, be used in groups to punch through the enemy front. Their tanks were accompanied by armored cars and motorcycles but did not depend directly upon the infantry. The German tactic, which became world-famous as the *Blitzkrieg* of the Second World War, was more successful in Spain than that of the Russians. This was probably owing to the fact that they supplied their own crews and communications teams, and that their Nationalist allies were generally better equipped than were the opposing troops. While the Republican soldiers learned to handle rifles, mortars and machine-guns as expertly as those of General Franco, they never achieved the same skill in field maneuvers. During the Second World War the same Russian tanks, leading Russian infantry, were to prove their worth in the great offensives of 1943 and 1944.

The Nationalists hurried to follow up their victory at Teruel with a general offensive toward the Levant and Catalonia. Along a north–south line, running roughly between Saragossa and Teruel, they concentrated well over 100,000 men, with avidly combative Spanish and Moroccan units in the lead. During the previous fifteen months they had amassed over 400 Italian and about 250 German planes, some 150 to 200 tanks and thousands of trucks. The greater part of these facilities was available for the offensive. In the air-dromes planes were drawn up wingtip to wingtip, and at the supply bases Ford, Studebaker, General Motors and Italian trucks stood hub to hub without fear of air raids.

The attack was launched on 9 March. Belchite and Quinto fell within the first twenty-four hours, and in a week the Nationalists had advanced an average of sixty miles all along the line. Tanks employing panzer tactics broke the front at selected points and en-circled the less mobile Republican troops, which were then bombed and strafed as they retreated from their fixed positions. Demoralized teenage conscripts cursed the government which was unable to provide them with adequate weapons and transportation, and sought cover in grain fields and orchards which had not been properly cultivated for many months. Meanwhile, in Saragossa exultant Nationalists bought images of the Virgin of Pilar mounted in shell

The Nationalist spearhead of tanks and armored
cars drove forward well in advance of the
infantry. *Right:* an armored-car commander
wearing the yoke and arrows, emblem of the
Falange; his vehicle is adorned with the figure of
Christ on the Cross. *Below:* tanks push ahead
through a village.

The chief objective of the raid on Barcelona was to terrorize the population of Republican Spain's largest city and to prove the efficiency and ruthlessness of Mussolini's air force. *Left:* one of the bombers. *Below:* aerial view of the bombardment of the dock area. *Opposite:* rescue work amid the rubble of the city.

casings, and young women of the Falange's Auxilio Social accompanied food trucks into the recently conquered towns.

On 11 March Hitler had occupied Austria, and a cabinet change in France had returned Léon Blum to the Premier's office. Prime Minister Negrín at once flew to Paris and convinced Blum temporarily to reopen the border, after which long-withheld Russian supplies began rapidly to pass from Bordeaux, Marseilles and Perpignan to Barcelona. Mussolini, acting on his own, ordered his Majorca-based bombers to strike at Barcelona, and the Italians raided the city eighteen times in forty-four hours, starting on the full moon night of 16 March. They employed two new types of bombs: a delayed-fuse weapon designed to pass through the roof and then explode inside a building, and a bomb which exploded with a strong lateral force so as to destroy things and persons within a few inches of the ground.

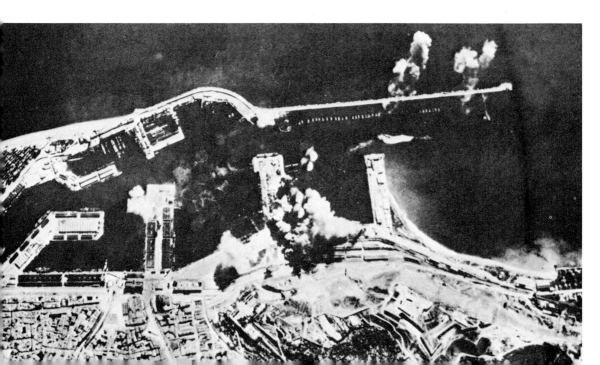

Mopping-up operations after the fall of Lérida to the Nationalist armies.

In Aragon the victorious offensive swept on. At the end of March, the 'El Campesino' division made a brief stand before the city of Lérida. When the Nationalists entered on 3 April they found only children and old women in the streets. One corps turned north following the river Segre into the Pyrenees and occupying the town of Tremp, whose water-power generators supplied Barcelona with most of its electricity. Other units rushed down the Ebro valley and on 15 April reached the small port of Viñaroz, thereby cutting off

Catalonia from the central and southern territories remaining in Republican hands. Thereafter, in the Maestrazgo, among mountains and olive groves where tanks were no longer effective, the advance met stiffening resistance; but by the end of the month the Nationalists held a strip of the Mediterranean coast running some fifty miles southward from the mouth of the river Ebro.

The Nationalists were supremely confident that the war would be over in a matter of days or weeks, and the military situation of the Republic was indeed desperate. Generals Rojo and Hidalgo de Cisneros talked of surrendering themselves to Franco as hostages for the broken Republican army, and the abject pessimism of the Defense Minister, Prieto, was notorious in government and diplomatic circles. But Negrín, counting on the new arms pouring over the French frontier, and convinced that at some point the Western democracies would have to stop appeasing the Fascist powers, was determined to fight on. He did not hesitate to browbeat President Azaña with a military demonstration in front of the presidential palace, and he demanded the resignation of his admired friend and colleague Prieto. Civilian morale was low, and grave food shortages developed as the Nationalists occupied large agricultural zones and as tens of thousands of new refugees crowded into the environs of Barcelona and Valencia. The conquering army had captured many prisoners, but there had been few desertions. Of some 5,000 soldiers who had retreated over the French border and been questioned by the French police, only about 250 chose to be repatriated to the Nationalist zone. The rest re-entered Catalonia. Negrín reorganized his cabinet, adding the Defense portfolio to his own duties. His Basque and Republican colleagues remained; Rojo and Hidalgo de Cisneros were ready to serve him as they had served Prieto. Army discipline generally continued to be strong. Fueled by Negrín's indomitable will to resist, the war would go on.

Resist! Resist! Stalin's watchword to Negrín. Nationalist caricature satirizing Negrín's dependence on the Soviet government.

Chapter Eight

INTERNATIONAL ASPECTS OF THE CIVIL WAR

Throughout 1937 and during the first months of 1938 (until the development of Hitler's threat to invade Czechoslovakia) the Spanish Civil War constituted the major foreign policy problem for the European powers. By the beginning of October 1936 the Insurgent navy had gained control both of the Mediterranean coasts close to Gibraltar and of the northern coast. In late October its destroyers were stopping Soviet freighters as they approached Valencia. During November and December the Italian and German

From the whole of Europe and the Americas volunteers came to fight, and die, for the Republican cause. These banners commemorate International Brigaders from Switzerland, France, Hungary, Italy, Czechoslovakia, England, Austria, Spain, Yugoslavia and Germany who were killed in Spain. Above the banners, Negrín's slogan is quoted: 'The blood which bathes our soil will bear fruit, it will not be lost, it will not be sterile.'

navies conferred several times concerning Spain, and made explicit agreements whereby Italy took the major share of responsibility for both surface and submarine operations in the Mediterranean, and Germany proposed primarily to protect her Atlantic shipping lanes to northern Spanish and Moroccan ports. On 17 November the Burgos government (on the eve of recognition by Germany and Italy) announced that it would sink ships carrying supplies to Republican ports. Claiming to be the only legal government of Spain it demanded 'belligerent rights' on the high seas, i.e. the right to stop and search ships of all nations, and to impose a blockade on enemy coasts. The granting of belligerent rights would also strongly imply diplomatic recognition by putting the Burgos and the Valencia governments on an equal footing so far as naval law was concerned. Neither the French nor the British were ready to recognize the Nationalist government in early 1937, and the British navy hoped to avoid unpleasant incidents by instructing its captains not to accompany merchant ships as far as Spanish territorial waters.

But widespread English sympathy for the Basques, together with enormous profits for the delivery of cargoes to Bilbao, undermined the official policy. British freighters delivered food and other supplies as the Basques prepared to defend themselves in early 1937. On 6 April the Nationalists announced a blockade of the Bilbao–Santander coast. The Basque government insisted that the blockade was a bluff, and that their shore-guns and armed trawlers could

protect any ship within the three-mile limit. Many voices in the British parliament questioned both the reality of the blockade and the propriety of the proud British navy permitting an unrecognized government to search British ships on the high seas. However, Franco's naval officers had solemnly assured their English counterparts that the blockade was effective. The English officers had solemnly assured the Baldwin government that the blockade was effective, and the cabinet had solemnly ordered British merchantmen not to try to sail to Bilbao. Then, on the night of 19–20 April, the *Seven Seas Spray*, carrying cargo from Valencia, entered Bilbao without interference, whereat the British government withdrew its order and occasional freighters docked in Bilbao until the city fell on 19 June.

The blockade question was thus settled without according belligerent rights to the Nationalists. More important and more dangerous to international peace was the question of attacks on merchant shipping in the Mediterranean. Italy was 'lending' several submarines and small destroyers to the Nationalist navy, and on 15 December 1936 the Soviet freighter *Komsomol* had been sunk off Cartagena. Altogether, from November 1936 until May 1937, the Nationalists and their Italo-German allies confiscated, damaged or sank about thirty-five ships, mostly British, Russian and Scandinavian. During late July and August 1936 the Republican navy had occasionally inconvenienced German freighters off the coast of Andalusia, but with this slight exception the Nationalists had been able to receive supplies and troops without interference at both their own and Portuguese ports.

During the same weeks as the controversy over the blockade of Bilbao, the Non-Intervention Committee was completing arrangements for land and sea surveillance of all Spanish frontiers. On 19 April the powers inaugurated a naval patrol which assigned the Mediterranean portion of the Republican coast to Italy and Germany, the Basque–Santander coast to England and the Franco zone coasts to France and England. There was to be no naval inspection of the Portuguese coast. Portugal would permit a few British observers on her Spanish frontier, and France would accept an international inspection of the Pyrenean frontier. These arrangements did not interfere in any way with attacks on ships approaching Republican ports in the Mediterranean, and in general confirmed the *de facto* situation in which the Republic was increasingly isolated while Nationalist Spain continued freely to import arms and men.

Concerned to maintain their rights as sovereign powers, neither the Republican nor the Nationalist governments recognized the establishment of the naval patrol, and the Republicans warned specifically that they would feel free to attack German and Italian warships entering their territorial waters. On 24 May Valencia planes bombed the Italian warship *Barletta* at Palma de Majorca, and the Italians announced that six officers had been killed. On 29 May

a similar raid struck the *Deutschland* in Ibiza harbor, killing twenty-two sailors. Germany accused the Soviets of causing the incident and the Burgos government interpreted the bombing as a desperate effort by Valencia to cause a general European war in order to stave off imminent defeat by the Nationalists. No one, however, really wanted a wider war. On 31 May the German navy shelled the port of Almería and then hastily announced that the incident was closed. She was still, however, seeking a plausible pretext to withdraw from the four-power naval patrol. On 15 June she claimed that the cruiser *Leipzig* had been torpedoed on the high seas. The Valencia government coupled its denial with an offer for the British navy to investigate the alleged incident. Germany haughtily refused the offer, and on 23 June Italy and Germany simultaneously announced their withdrawal from the patrol, made necessary, as they put it, by the piratical conduct of the 'Red' government. The Portuguese then asked the British to recall their frontier observers, and on 12 July the French withdrew observer facilities along the Pyrenees while continuing to keep the frontier closed.

During July and August 1937 about twenty-five to thirty ships were bombed or torpedoed in the Mediterranean by officially 'unknown' (but clearly known to be Italian) submarines. Of these a dozen were Spanish, eight were British, and two were Russian. The appeasement-minded government of Neville Chamberlain had been trying to mollify the Axis powers ever since the *Deutschland* bombing, but Mussolini's present audacity was too much. It was one thing for the German-Italian Axis openly to arm the Nationalists, it was another for Italy to act as a law unto herself in international waters of great consequence to Great Britain. The British called a conference of all countries bordering the Mediterranean, inviting them to Nyon in Switzerland to discuss the problem of 'unknown submarines' and 'piracy.' Germany and Italy blandly responded with the suggestion that the matter be discussed by the Non-Intervention Committee, but the aroused British indicated on this occasion that they were in earnest. The conference was convened at Nyon on 10 September (despite the ostentatious absence of Italy) and it took the British less than thirty-six hours to make their policy clear. They announced that the British and French navies would together patrol the entire Mediterranean, and that any unidentified submarine would be sunk on sight. The mysterious torpedoings ceased, and Italy even joined the new patrol on her own request; also, very few Russian ships sailed for Spain after August 1937. So in this particular comedy Great Britain and Italy both got what they most wanted: Italy had largely cut off Russian aid to the Republic; Great Britain had acted firmly as a Mediterranean power and had, by her silence on all but the piracy issue, signaled to Italy that she did not object to open Italian aid to Burgos.

In the months following Nyon, Chamberlain was anxious to conclude a naval agreement with Italy. While negotiations proceeded, the Italians behaved themselves, with the brief exception of a torpedo attack on the British freighter *Endymion* on 11 February 1938. The agreement was signed on 16 April, the day after General Alonso Vego had reached the Mediterranean, and when it appeared that the Nationalists were about to win the war quickly. Between mid-April and the end of June Mussolini and Franco tweaked the lion's tail by bombing some 22 British ships, 11 of which were sunk or disabled. From July until October another 21 British ships were hit, and fifteen similar attacks were reported in January and February of 1939, the last months of the war. From time to time the British submitted damage claims to Burgos. The Nationalists could barely conceal their scorn for a government which obviously desired their victory but which simultaneously demanded compensation for the damage done to British ships carrying cargoes for the Republic.

Closely intertwined with Great Power naval negotiations was the question of foreign troops. From the beginning of the war Franco had depended upon thousands of Moorish mercenaries, and the Republic had recruited dozens of foreign pilots and had welcomed thousands of volunteer soldiers. Almost from the first days of the war Left-Socialists and anarchists had urged that Spanish Morocco be offered independence. In their view the Moroccan protectorate was a vestige of colonialism which the Republic ought long since to have liquidated, and such action now might interfere with the Insurgents' recruitment of Moorish troops. In February 1937 the Caballero government hinted through diplomatic channels that it would gladly offer Spanish Morocco to England and France if they would oblige Germany and Italy to desist from aiding the Nationalists. These

Look, a Spaniard! Cartoon from *La Vanguardia.*

feelers elicited no response, and in April the Burgos press published the story. The entire clumsy effort testified to the diplomatic isolation of the Republic, and while there is very little evidence available today concerning politics within Spanish Morocco after July 1936, it is clear that General Franco continued to recruit Moors with the assistance of local tribal authorities.★

This group of Nationalist soldiers, taken prisoner by the Republicans, consisted of (from left to right) two Falangists, two German aviators, one Moor, two Falangists and four Italians.

By March 1937 the Nationalist forces included tens of thousands of Moors, 70,000 Italians, some 5,000 Germans and an undetermined number, probably several thousands, of Portuguese. On the Republican side there were approximately 35,000 foreigners in the International Brigades and about 2,000 Soviet technicians and staff officers. After the massive import of Moorish and Italian troops had been accomplished, the Non-Intervention Committee on 20 February 1937 announced a ban on the recruitment of non-Spanish soldiers. In early February Franco and his allies were confident that these reinforcements would conquer Madrid and end the war. But unfortunately the Moors were decimated at the Jarama and the Italians were beaten at Guadalajara in mid-March. Thus on 23 March Count Grandi, the Italian ambassador in London, expressed the true sentiments of his government (while technically exceeding his instructions) by announcing that not a single Italian volunteer would leave until the war was won.

★ Recent research by Professor Charles R. Haldtead indicates that the Nationalist army included 70,000–80,000 Moors from late 1937 to the end of the war.

Foreign intervention. *Above:* Moorish troops take part in a ceremonial parade. *Below:* a detachment of Carlist volunteers.

They tell me Germany and Italy are helping Franco. If I had proof I'd believe it. Republican cartoon attacking Great Britain's failure to move against Axis aid to the Nationalists and to enforce the non-intervention policy fairly.

From early 1937 until October 1938 the Non-Intervention Committee wrestled with the problem of foreign troops. There were several almost insuperable obstacles. The Committee tried to side-step all significant definitions by using the term 'volunteer' for all categories of foreigner. The vast majority of Franco's foreigners were uniformed soldiers who by and large enjoyed their assignment, but who were in no ordinary sense of the word volunteers. The majority of the International Brigades were indeed volunteers, many of whom had escaped from Fascist concentration camps or had left their civilian jobs (and passports) behind them when they came to fight for the Republic. But there were also the 2,000 Soviet technicians and the hundreds of Comintern agents who could hardly be called volunteers. A second obstacle was the steadfast refusal of the Nationalists ever to recognize that there were at least four times as many foreigners in their ranks as in those of the Republic. Furthermore, at all times General Franco protested against the discussion as an infringement on the sovereign rights of Nationalist Spain. Most important in his objections was the unacknowledged fact that he could never win the war if all foreign troops were to be withdrawn.

On 14 July 1937 (while the Battle of Brunete was raging) England offered a plan whereby, in return for making 'substantial progress' in the withdrawal of volunteers, each side would receive belligerent rights. The Republicans considered that they, as the legitimate government, already enjoyed belligerent rights, so that part of the plan could benefit only the Nationalists. They, and their Italian and German allies, could also haggle indefinitely over the meaning of 'substantial.' In the hope of avoiding this sort of useless debate the Soviets steadily demanded that *all* foreign volunteers be withdrawn before belligerent rights were granted. In the fall of 1937 the Italians said they would be willing to discuss the withdrawal of an equal number from each side, an arrangement which would have favored the Nationalists by a ratio of four to one. Early in 1938 there was talk of proportional withdrawals. The Anglo-Italian Agreement of 16 April made ratification of the naval clauses dependent on 'substantial withdrawal' of Italian troops. Into the summer there was much palaver about how to count the volunteers, how to pay for their repatriation, to what ports to ship them, etc. By August a revised plan calling for proportionate withdrawals was ready. On 16 August (during the Battle of the Ebro) Franco announced his acceptance 'in principle,' while continuing to protest against the infringement of sovereignty. And he attached two conditions: that belligerent rights be granted *before* the withdrawal started, and that an equal number be withdrawn from each side. The deadlock was never resolved, but in late September the Republic unilaterally announced the dissolution and repatriation of the International Brigades. In October, shortly after the Munich Pact, 10,000 Italians were repatriated, but since 2,400 had arrived in July and 9,000 more were to be sent in the first three months of 1939, this repatriation did not substantially reduce the size of the Italian contingent in Nationalist Spain.★

Payment for supplies was another matter of intense international interest. The Republic's main supplier from October 1936 until late 1937 was the Soviet Union. At the end of October the Madrid government sent more than half the Bank of Spain's gold reserve to Odessa in four unescorted Russian freighters. The monetary value of this shipment was about $518,000,000 (figured at $35 per ounce). It was used to pay for Soviet arms and other military supplies, and ever since 1939 the Soviets have claimed that their deliveries to Republican Spain more than exhausted the value of the gold they received in advance payment. The Republic bought elsewhere in Europe, largely on the black market of 'surplus' First World War and 1920s equipment, most of it French and British, some of it' German and Czech. Catalan businessmen and Comintern agents arranged the most important deals. One country sent food and small arms without attaching any political or financial conditions: the Mexican Republic whose President was Lázaro Cárdenas.

On the Nationalist side a mixed Italian-Spanish trading company, SAFNI, was organized in August 1936 to handle the pyrites, olive oil and woollens which Spain was to exchange for military supplies. Reports in mid-1937 indicated that the Italians were getting little in return for the arms delivered thus far, and at times Mussolini threatened to curtail exports, but he did not carry out such threats, nor did Italy ever recover any sizable proportion of her investment in the Nationalist victory.

★ I owe these statistics, and a few earlier figures on the Italians, to the courtesy of Professor John Coverdale, author of a forthcoming study of Italian intervention in Spain.

Payment for German aid was placed on a strict business basis within ten days of the start of the war. A bi-national trading company, HISMA/ROWAK, was established under the leadership of Johannes Bernhardt, the Nazi businessman who had long been established in Tetuán and who had communicated to Hitler Franco's first request for aircraft. The Rif mines were requisitioned from their French and British owners and HISMA, as of January 1937, held a contract to deliver to Germany 60 per cent of the Rio Tinto production at 42 pesetas to the pound – the exchange rate set by General Franco. For cash transactions HISMA maintained a large peseta credit, and ROWAK had a Mark balance in Berlin. The company held a monopoly under the supervision of the two governments. In addition to ore, it dealt in wheat, hides and vegetables.

The Germans were even more concerned with postwar advantages than with immediate payment. Until late 1938 General Franco very cannily resisted their efforts, reiterating in all conversations that his was only a provisional government which could not dispose of the national patrimony. Existing Spanish law limited foreign capital to a 25 per cent share in Spanish enterprises. In March 1938 he conceded a new upper limit of 40 per cent. On 19 November 1938, when he needed massive quantities of arms for the projected Catalan offensive, and after Hitler had won his greatest peace-time triumph at Munich, Franco consented to the creation of MONTANA, a consolidation of five peninsular mining companies, in the three largest of which the Germans would hold 75 per cent of the capital.

With this important exception, the Generalissimo maintained his economic independence throughout the war. After the fall of Bilbao in June 1937, he unabashedly directed the lion's share of Biscayan ore to its traditional British market, despite the displeasure of the Germans. Finding American vehicles more to his taste than German and Italian ones, he used his foreign exchange earnings to buy 1,200 Fiat trucks, 1,800 German trucks and 12,000 Ford, Studebaker and General Motor trucks. Nothing better illustrates the successful trading policies of Nationalist Spain than the fact that in 1937 their exports to the sterling area were worth $60,000,000 and to Germany $31,000,000, making a total of $91,000,000, whereas the entire exports of undivided Spain in 1935 had amounted to only $115,000,000. Confidence in Franco and his eventual victory on the part of foreign businessmen was such that he did not need to float any international loans in order to finance the war. His commercial debts by the end of 1938 were estimated at anywhere from $100,000,000 to $200,000,000, the large German and Italian portions of which were to be automatically canceled by the Axis defeat in the Second World War.

As we have seen, the policies of the major powers toward the Spanish Civil War had already been established by late October 1936, and these policies were carried out fairly consistently throughout the struggle. Besides the military and economic intervention discussed above, there were several other factors which played a proportionately minor but still significant role in the international politics of the war. One of these was the attitude of the Roman Catholic Church. The sacking of churches and the murder of priests in the first weeks of the war had brought the Spanish priesthood to the side of the Insurgents in a simple reflex of self-defense. The Primate, Cardinal Gomá, was a fanatical anti-Marxist and had for several years been an open admirer of Fascism. But the situation of the Church was complicated by the fact that many military and Falangist leaders were anticlerical, and that the Basque Nationalists were siding with the Republic. On 6 August 1936 Cardinal Gomá issued a pastoral letter supporting the military rising, but it was common knowledge in Bilbao that the bishops of Pamplona and Vitoria had objected strenuously to much of the phrasing. During October 1936 the military, in their rage against the 'anti-national' (meaning anti-Castilian-military) Basques, had executed a dozen Basque priests for 'espionage.' The fall of Bilbao eliminated all hesitation on the part of the Vatican, which up to that time had refused unequivocally to support Burgos. On 1 July 1937 the Spanish bishops issued a collective letter fully justifying and supporting the Nationalist cause. But during the spring hundreds of Basque children had been sent to foster-homes in France and England. Spanish Catholic authorities had bristled at the notion that these children would be better cared for abroad than in Spain, and the children's terror-stricken reactions to the sight of airplanes had not improved the international reputation of the Franquist military.

The bishops bless the Nationalist cause. Flanked by senior army officers, a group of clerics gives the Fascist salute.

The Pope: 'I give you my blessing in the name of Mohammed and Luther.' Republican satire on the Vatican's support for the Nationalist cause.

The Republican government attempted conscientiously to improve the position of practicing Catholics in its zone. On 7 August 1937 it decreed freedom of private Catholic worship, and from early in 1937 the Basque Minister of Justice, Manuel de Irujo, arranged the release from prison of many priests held solely because of their clerical affiliation. During 1938 Mass was said in a number of Republican army units, and from October 1938 the Basques were permitted to celebrate services publicly in Barcelona. But these relatively small accomplishments, on an issue of great consequence for international opinion, only served to underline how bitterly anti-Catholic were the operative political forces (and probably public opinion) in the Republican zone. The Vatican, by sending a nuncio to Salamanca in October 1937, indicated its ready acceptance of the Nationalists as the future rulers of Spain.

Another issue of considerable international import arose from the fact that during the first weeks of the war several thousand people had taken refuge in foreign embassy buildings in Madrid. Contemporary European, British and United States practice did not include the right of political refuge in diplomatic premises. The British and United States embassies received instructions not to admit refugees of Spanish nationality on the grounds that this would constitute intervention in the internal affairs of a friendly power. In Latin America the right to political asylum in foreign embassies was a time-honored custom, but it was understood as applying to leaders of governments overthrown by revolution or to prominent personalities belonging to persecuted political parties. None of those seeking refuge in the Madrid embassies were leaders of an overturned régime and only a small minority were leaders of anti-government parties. The refugees included the families of many moderate political and business figures who felt threatened by the wave of political assassinations; they also included large numbers of army officers and civil servants who expected a quick Insurgent victory. Most of the diplomatic corps were favorable to the rising. The Peruvian and Cuban legations were known centers of espionage. The Dutch and Norwegian chargés d'affaires were both pro-Nazi German citizens. The Turkish, Polish, Finnish, Dutch, Norwegian and Belgian embassies rented extra buildings in order to expand their refugee facilities; and the Republican government, unable to control its own terrorist partisans during the first three months of the war, frequently aided people to reach the relative safety of the embassies.

As the war lengthened, the crowded legations became an embarrassment, not to say a scandal. At night, shots were sometimes fired from embassy buildings. Food and luxuries entered duty-free. In 1937 the residents were eating better than most Madrileños, and some of them were engaged in a highly lucrative black market. With order having been restored in the street, friends and families could visit freely, bringing information of military value which could then be sent to Salamanca in the diplomatic mail pouches, or broadcast with impunity from transmitters located in the legations. In the spring of 1937 the Caballero government wanted the embassies emptied as completely as possible, but it also wanted guarantees that several thousand men of military age would not take arms against the Republic. The Foreign Minister, Álvarez del Vayo, negotiated separate agreements with France, Holland, Turkey, Czechoslovakia and Cuba, whereby Spain agreed to evacuate the refugees and the contracting government undertook to keep the men from emigrating to Nationalist Spain. Most governments honored their pledges, but the Belgians released their contingent unconditionally as soon as they had stepped on French soil, thereby delaying considerably the arrangement of further evacuations.

Altogether some 15,000 to 20,000 people sought refuge at one moment or another, the majority of them for short periods during the first three months of the war. In late June 1937 the government stated that 4,000 people had been evacuated, but this figure gives only a minimal indication since many entries and exits were made without record. Toward the end of the war the total refugee population stood at 2,000 to 3,000. The publicity arising from the embassy question was generally unfavorable to the Republic. The origin of the problem was a constant reminder of the government's helplessness during the first weeks of the war. Later newspaper interviews and letters widely published by the refugees in Europe and Latin America highlighted the ugly situation within Madrid during the summer of 1936 and reinforced conservative preference for the Nationalists as the 'forces of order.' At the same time the Republic received little credit for permitting a practice of asylum which had absolutely no counterpart in Nationalist Spain.

All the wartime Republican governments cooperated willingly in the efforts of the International Red Cross to arrange the exchange of non-combatants, hostages and prisoners of war. In mid-September 1936 Dr Marcel Junod of the IRC negotiated a proposal to exchange 130 women and children between Bilbao and Burgos. His efforts were enthusiastically supported by both the Giral cabinet and the Basque autonomous government. On 27 September the Basques delivered their 130 prisoners, but the Burgos authorities informed Dr Junod (after a banquet in his honor) that the Basque women in question had already been freed and did not wish to return to Bilbao. It took six more weeks of bargaining, and the aid of highly placed Carlists, finally to obtain 40 Basque children as the counterpart of the 130 people originally turned over by the Basques. Despite the gross inequality of this first exchange the Largo Caballero government in March 1937 agreed to Dr Junod's proposal to reopen negotiations with the Nationalists through the good offices of General Franco's brother-in-law, Ramón Serrano Súñer. The long discussions were inevitably hampered by widely differing criteria for the legal treatment of combatant prisoners. On 9 April the Caballero government decreed that henceforth prisoners were not to be court-martialed except by specific order of the cabinet. Caballero issued only two such orders during his remaining weeks in office, and not more than a few dozen were issued by Prime Minister Negrín during the following year. However, prisoners in the Nationalist zone were regularly court-martialed, considerable numbers being condemned

Young refugees, the children of Spanish Communists, are welcomed on their arrival in Moscow.

to death and a large proportion receiving twenty- to thirty-year sentences. When the two governments bargained over their lists of captives, the Nationalists insisted that they could not exchange men convicted of serious crimes for simple prisoners. The first actual exchanges did not occur until October 1937. Almost all the agreements involved named individuals or small groups, and by the end of the war only 647 prisoners had been handed over to the International Red Cross by each side. In late 1936 the Republicans had permitted the IRC delegates to aid the widows of men who had been assassinated during the first weeks of the war, and throughout the conflict they facilitated the emigration of non-combatants. These policies were not reciprocated in the Nationalist zone, where the authorities never admitted that innocent people had been assassinated, where the IRC delegates faced strong prejudices because they were Protestants, and where many officers identified them simplistically as 'international' and 'red.'

The IRC had hoped that the Spanish Civil War might furnish the occasion to extend to civil wars the accepted Hague and Geneva Convention rules concerning treatment of prisoners in international conflicts. But these rules, governing exchange of medical personnel, regular visits to prisons and the submission of complete lists of prisoners, were not accepted by either side. On the other hand, both camps permitted the IRC to establish a message service whereby families could learn whether their sons and brothers were still alive. Some three million requests for information and two million responses were transmitted via Geneva in the course of the war. An unfortunate aspect of the IRC efforts, in terms of Spanish public feeling, was the fact that the vast majority of those exchanged were foreigners: Italian and German aviators, Russian sailors and pilots and members of the International Brigades. Also, since both sides wished to avoid offending foreign powers unnecessarily, non-Spanish prisoners enjoyed a better prison régime than did Spaniards.

It was a matter of great importance for both governments to avoid undue political influence in their internal affairs by those allies on whom they depended for armaments. Because of their overwhelming dependence on the Soviet Union, the problem was more difficult for the Republicans. During 1936–38 Stalin was following two contradictory policies. On the one hand, in the search for 'collective security,' he wanted to restrain social revolution and reassure both the Spanish middle classes and the parliamentary governments of France and Britain. On the other hand, he was pursuing a merciless vendetta against potential and imaginary opponents in the world Communist movement. He and his lieutenants in Spain (the most important of whom were not Spaniards) therefore proclaimed the defense of bourgeois democracy against a militarist-Fascist rebellion, and allied themselves with middle-class Republicans and right-wing Socialists. They supported Largo Caballero while they thought they could manage him, and then undermined him when he refused to confirm their domination of the political commissariat in the Republican army and when he opposed their efforts to eliminate the anarchists and the anti-Stalinist Left. From May 1937 to the end of the war they supported Juan Negrín in all his military policies and in his prodigious, though unsuccessful, efforts to get the Western powers to reverse the non-intervention policy. They also accepted his refusal in 1937 to merge the Socialist and Communist Parties and his release in late 1938 of various imprisoned POUM leaders whom they had characterized as 'Trotskyite-Fascist vermin.'

But in the very first weeks of Negrín's prime ministership the Communists created an international scandal through the kidnapping and murder of Andrés Nin. Nin had been a major figure in the factional politics of the Communist International in the 1920s. He had been a friend and at times a close collaborator of Leon Trotsky, and this relationship had caused Stalin to veto his nomination as Secretary-General of the Spanish Communist Party in 1927. He had become one of the founders, and the leading theoretician, of the POUM. He had served briefly as Minister of Justice in the Catalan autonomous government in late 1936, and he had been arrested in June 1937 with other POUM leaders during the repression which followed the Barcelona street fighting of May. Nin was never heard from again. Questions from his friends and from international reporters were evaded by a government which itself probably did not know exactly what had happened. Six weeks later, in early August, it was public knowledge that Nin had been removed from the Barcelona government prison to a secret Communist prison near Alcalá de Henares, that his captors had sought unavailingly to extract a confession of the type being used in the Moscow purge trials, and that he had then been murdered. The Communists claimed that he had escaped to Berlin via the Franco zone! Negrín had to choose between public condemnation of the assassination and Soviet military aid, although the latter was about to be much reduced in any case. In order to maintain the military chances of the Spanish Republic he swallowed his anger.

General Franco was by no means spared from crude pressures on the part of his allies. Both the German bombing of Guernica and the Italian bombings of Barcelona were decided without his knowledge. The island of Majorca was virtually an Italian colony during the war. Germany and Italy pressed their strategic views in ways that undermined Franco's prestige at home, and the German ambassador in early 1937 dabbled in the internal politics of the Falange. From time to time the world press reported scuffles between Italian and Spanish soldiers, and Germany in 1938 was making economic demands which certainly infringed on Spanish sovereignty. But the Axis rulers did not have a political party and press of their own in Nationalist Spain, and at no time did they attempt to exercise any such political influence as that of Stalin in the internal politics of the Republican zone.

General Franco takes the salute at his victory parade in Madrid, 18 May 1939.

Chapter Nine

FROM POLITICAL CONSOLIDATION
TO NATIONALIST VICTORY

During the first months of 1938 General Franco devoted a great deal of attention to the establishment of a regular government and to the publication of decree-laws which would set the direction of development for postwar Spain. The Fascist corporate model of his principal ally was available, and he borrowed some of its trappings, but he did not view Spain through Fascist eyes. Rather he saw her situation as in many ways parallel to the situation which had existed at the beginning of the reign of the Catholic Kings, Ferdinand and Isabella. Much as had been the case in 1474, the Spain of 1938 was divided by religious dissension and civil disorder. Previous governments had squandered the national heritage, in the fifteenth century by granting royal lands to the factious nobility, under the Republic by granting unwise land reforms and provincial statutes of autonomy. The General was a pragmatic ruler. He did not think that the exiled King Alfonso could play the role of Queen Isabella. He restored the former monarch's citizenship and returned to him the family properties, but he left for the future the question of a restoration.

On 3 January Franco formed a cabinet which reflected accurately the various political currents within Nationalist Spain. There were three monarchists who had held important offices before the coming of the Republic: General Gómez Jordana, the generally pro-British Foreign Minister, Andrés Amado, Minister of Finance, and Pedro Sáinz Rodríguez, Minister of Education. A leading Carlist, the Count of Rodezno, served as Minister of Justice. There were two Falangists: the charter member Raimundo Fernández Cuesta, a recently exchanged prisoner from the Republican zone, who became Secretary-General of the party; and the less well-known González Bueno who served as Minister of Labor. General Dávila, successor to Mola as commander of the northern army, and unconditionally devoted to the Caudillo, became Minister of the Army. The elderly General Martínez Anido, who had acquired a ferocious reputation for his repression of the Barcelona anarchists in the early

A ceremony of loyalty in a Burgos hotel. Guests salute a portrait of General Franco after hearing the news of a Nationalist victory.

1920s, and who had served Primo de Rivera as Minister of the Interior, now became Minister of Public Order. Ramón Serrano Súñer, Franco's brother-in-law and close adviser, a brilliant lawyer and an ardent Catholic who had once headed the CEDA youth organization, served as Minister of the Interior. Juan Antonio Suances, a boyhood friend of Franco's and a successful industrialist, was appointed as Minister of Commerce and Industry. The new cabinet took the oath of office in the centuries-old monastery of Las Huelgas, near Burgos, in a ceremony redolent of late medieval Castilian royalty, and described by Serrano Súñer as 'intimate, fervent, devout, like a vigil in arms.'

Several fundamental laws were published during the spring. On 9 March came the Labor Charter, governing wages and working conditions in industry and protecting the leases of tenant farmers. It did not, however, apply to wage laborers on the great estates. In April the government created the Servicio Nacional de Reforma

Económica Social de la Tierra. The Republic had distributed some half-million acres to the peasants before the war, and several million additional acres were being operated as cooperative or collective farms by early 1938. The task of the new Servicio would be to return the property to its rightful owners and to substitute for Republican and revolutionary land reform an unspecified form of 'colonization.' On 5 April the Catalan autonomy statute of 1932 was abrogated, and on 22 April a law of press censorship was announced. On 3 May the Jesuits, referred to as a particularly Spanish Order, were welcomed back to Spain, and their property, most of which had been held for them since 1932 by other Orders and by fictitious corporations, was restored.

The government worked positively to revive the influence of the Church, an influence which had admittedly been diminishing rapidly for decades before the coming of the Republic. Crucifixes were to hang in every secondary and university classroom, and the image of the Virgin was to be present in every primary class. Attendance at religious services was required of all civil and military officials, and religious instruction in both primary and secondary schools became obligatory everywhere except in Morocco. All schoolteachers were examined as to their religious beliefs, and many schools were closed for lack of instructors with satisfactory religious qualifications. The Republican divorce law, already abrogated in practice, was officially repealed in March 1938. The entire corpus of decree-laws confirmed existing trends toward a centralized state, a government-controlled economy and the restoration of vested economic and religious interests of the pre-Republican era. The Labor Charter alone paid mild lip-service to the ideals of the Falange Left.

This government, which appealed to the conservative élite and which rested on bayonets, was firm but hardly popular. Many in the Falange wanted the blood letting terminated, and feared the exploitation of their country by foreigners. On 19 April, anniversary of the forced unification of the Falange, General Yagüe caused a considerable stir in Burgos by demanding genuine social reform, calling for the release of thousands held in prisoner-of-war camps, and recognizing the bravery and sincerity of the Republican army. On several occasions during the spring the discreet and cautious German ambassador von Stohrer reported to his government that there were still guerrillas operating in the Asturias, that the 'reds' would win any referendum on the future government of Spain, that England and France must not be given any opportunity to mediate, and that large new quantities of German and Italian aid would be necessary even after the victorious offensive which had reached the Mediterranean in April.

In Republican Spain Prime Minister Negrín personified the will to resist. Having persuaded Léon Blum to reopen the frontier in mid-March, and having convinced a number of French military officials

Juan Negrín, Republican Minister from May 1937 to the end of the war. A physiologist of international reputation and right wing Socialist, he incarnated the Republican will to resist.

that their self-interest required the survival of the Spanish Republic, he reorganized his own cabinet in April. The resignation of Prieto ended 'defeatism' at the Ministry of Defense, and the reduced role of Catalan and Basque representatives increased Negrín's personal control of Republican resources; but it also increased Communist influence just at the time when it was most essential to obtain a change of policy on the part of the Western democratic powers. In a maximum effort to achieve the latter aim, and also to answer the reactionary decrees being published in Nationalist Spain, Negrín on 1 May delivered one of his rare public speeches. In the form of 'thirteen points' he listed his conditions for ending the Civil War, the chief of which were: maintenance of Spanish integrity from both military and economic penetration; a plebiscite on the form of a new republic once the fighting ceased; regional liberties and individual freedom of conscience; agrarian reform, with respect for small property; no confiscation of foreign businesses whose owners were not implicated in the rebellion; a general political amnesty; affirmation of Spain's historic support of the League of Nations; and adherence to 'collective security' within the League framework.

During April and May up to 25,000 tons of new war supplies crossed the frontier at Cerbère, in French trucks whose drivers worked for low pay, but who were partisans of the Republic and who could reward themselves materially by buying up furs and watches at bargain prices in the Catalan towns. Most important of the new imports were about 200 heavy field guns and 100 crated I-16 'Ratas,' the best Russian fighter planes, some of them with mountings for four machine-guns (instead of the usual two). French cabinet changes in April reduced the proportion of pro-Republican members, and Mussolini was threatening direct action if the frontier was not closed again. In late May the Nationalist air force machine-gunned several French truck convoys as a warning. The Soviets, who with renewed hope for collective security had half a dozen freighters *en route* for Havre and Marseilles, urged France to resist the pressure for closure, but by early June the French had once again virtually sealed the frontier. Inside Spain the civilian population suffered from food shortages and general war-weariness, but the army, which had maintained discipline even in the disastrous retreat to the sea, responded strongly to new arms from Russia and France, and to vigorous new leadership from Negrín.

Working in intimate collaboration, the Prime Minister and his chief of staff, General Vicente Rojo, sought a field of battle which would strike at the communications of the Nationalist army, place the fighting in hill country so as to minimize the enemy's material superiority and yet enable the Republic to concentrate its reserves and supplies. They chose the bend of the Ebro river, between Fayón and Benifollet, an area held by one division of General Yagüe's Moroccan army. North of this bend they concentrated about 100,000 men, slightly over 100 operational planes and 100 heavy guns and several dozen light anti-aircraft pieces. In early July the troops (frequently visited by the Prime Minister) were rehearsing the use of pontoon bridges and small boats. Their training anticipated the fact that communications with the rear would be extremely difficult, and that machine-guns and mortars would have to do most of the work usually assigned to field artillery.

Once again achieving complete surprise in their initiative, the Republicans began to cross the Ebro on the night of 24 July. In the course of a week some 50,000 men under the field command of the Communist Colonel José Modesto occupied the hills south of the river. During the day the Republicans used their newly arrived 'Ratas' and their entire anti-aircraft artillery to protect the narrow bridges against Nationalist bombers. Most of the supplies, however, crossed by night. The Nationalists opened the dams along the Pyrenean tributaries of the Ebro, and these floodwaters descended to the battle area, temporarily destroying the pontoons. General

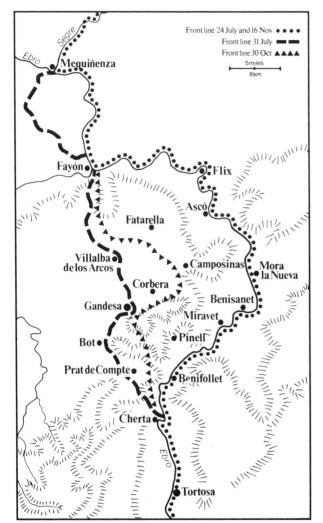

Map of the battle of the river Ebro, showing the fluctuations of the battle-fronts. The sketch on the right illustrates the rapid progress of Franco's final thrust forward in Catalonia from positions established during the fighting in the summer and fall of 1938.

Franco, responding as always to a local challenge, rushed up reinforcements, with the result that by 1 August the advance had been stopped just short of the towns of Gandesa and Villalba de los Arcos. The army dug in, using wells for command posts and stone parapets for cover. The country was hilly, with few trees. The ground was hard, and the bombers came over hourly; still the infantry dug shallow but carefully zigzagged trenches, often at intervals of only ten yards.

The initial success of the crossing raised the prestige of Negrín, but when the advance had been halted, and it became evident that the bulk of the Republican army might be trapped and annihilated with its back to the river, criticism of the Prime Minister became stronger than ever. Knowing that President Azaña wished to form a peace cabinet under the moderate Socialist Julián Besteiro, Negrín precipitated a cabinet crisis himself with a decree placing all Catalan military factories under the jurisdiction of the Communist-controlled subsecretariat of armament. Azaña was intimidated by an air force demonstration over Barcelona and by thousands of telegrams from the front demanding the retention of Negrín. He yielded, and on 16 August Negrín retained his office, making only unimportant shifts in the composition of his third cabinet.

In the hills above Gandesa the Nationalists now held the initiative. They prepared their counterattacks with all-day artillery barrages from guns lined up hub to hub as in the great Western-front battles of the First World War; and they supplemented the artillery with relays of bombers. But when the infantry rushed forward they were met by murderous fire from machine-guns and mortars. The battle continued in this manner for ninety days, during which time the Nationalists achieved a maximum penetration of five miles along a twenty-mile front. General Franco was impatient at the slow progress of the counteroffensive. The air force protested at the use of their bombers as artillery, and the Italians sulked in their tents. The eager young 'provisional second lieutenants' whose boyish heroics had been the despair of their German training officers now died leading gallant charges against the stubborn (and equally teenage) units of a Republican army which by all the rules had been beaten, but which did not know it.

From Barcelona journalists of international reputation, such as Herbert L. Matthews, Vincent Sheehan, Lawrence Fernsworth, Louis Fischer and 'Pertinax,' all reported the moderate, Western orientation of the Negrín government and wrote admiringly of both Republican military recovery and civil administration. Prominent conservatives in the Anglo-Saxon world, notably Winston Churchill and the former U.S. Secretary of State, Henry L. Stimson, declared themselves favorable to the Republic in the summer of 1938. In early September Negrín flew to Switzerland, ostensibly to attend an international medical congress, in reality to make a supreme effort to achieve a compromise peace at a secret meeting with the leading Nationalist diplomat, the Duke of Alba.

That meeting, like other peace feelers of the previous six months, was fruitless, given the determination of General Franco to refuse all compromise. But the military fate of the Republic was now destined to be settled as the by-product of a larger international crisis. Hitler had no sooner swallowed Austria than he demanded of Czechoslovakia all the areas which in his view were inhabited by oppressed ethnic Germans: areas which happened to contain all of Czechoslovakia's defensive fortifications. During August and September Britain had pressed the Czechs to concede Hitler's entire demands, but on 22 September, in a personal meeting, the Führer had suddenly posed new conditions which were too much even for the appeasement-minded Prime Minister Chamberlain, and the latter did not protest when the Czechs decreed general mobilization. It appeared that war was inevitable. The Verdun-like resistance in the hills above the Ebro would now be rewarded, for if the Soviets and the Western powers joined in a war of defense against Hitlerite aggression, the Republic would be a recognized member of the anti-Fascist coalition. During the last ten days of September General Franco hastened to assure London and Paris that he would be absolutely neutral in case of war. To his great relief the Prime Ministers of Great Britain, France, Italy and Germany met at Munich on 28 September. Without consulting the Soviet Union they delivered the entire fortified zone of Czechoslovakia to Hitler.

The Munich Pact was a death blow to the diplomatic hopes of the Spanish Republic. For another month its troops hung on grimly in the Sierra de Gandesa, but in the first fifteen days of November they had to evacuate what was left of their salient, having lost at least 40,000 dead and wounded, together with the overwhelming bulk of the guns and planes which had crossed the French border between 13 March and 2 June. The international war scare in September had cut the flow of German and Italian supplies to the Nationalists, and Franco's statements of neutrality had not endeared him to Hitler and Mussolini. However, in late November the signing of the German-Spanish economic agreement was followed by renewed imports of war *matériel*. On 23 December General Franco launched his final, decisive offensive against the Republican army in Catalonia. A force of 350,000 men attacked along the entire Segre–Ebro line from Lérida to Tortosa. They had a field-gun for every ten yards of front, unchallenged control of the skies and sufficient transport to allow the advancing troops to be relieved every forty-eight hours in any sector where they encountered strong resistance. In their path lay 90,000

The Catalan Offensive. Bombing Republican trenches in the vineyards.

Above: Republican soldiers taken prisoner during the Nationalist advance.
Below: Generals Yagüe and Asensio, victorious conquerors of Barcelona.
After the fall of the Catalan capital, on 22 January 1939, only the central
zone, bounded approximately by Madrid, Valencia and Almería, remained
in Republican hands.

Almost half a million people fled before the advancing Nationalist troops, fearful of a peace of victorious revenge. *Above:* a column of troops marches into exile. *Opposite:* civilians, carrying a few possessions, cross the border into France.

semi-armed men whose morale and supplies had been exhausted by the Battle of the Ebro. Only the crack Communist-led units of Lister, Galán and Tagüeña offered serious resistance. On 15 January the Nationalists entered Tarragona without a fight.

The government talked half-heartedly of turning Barcelona into a second Madrid, but an irresistible panic seized the population of Catalonia and half a million human beings began trudging toward the French border. The government released its several thousand political prisoners. Those of the Left joined the retreat to France; those of the Right were protected by police and the International Red Cross delegates. A few lynchings occurred, at the time of each defeat and prison opening. For the most part the city and its officials passively awaited the Nationalist arrival. On 22 December General Yagüe's troops began to occupy the metropolis, almost without firing a shot. The doctors of the Nationalist army found the hospital patients unfed for two or three days past, and did their best to protect the wounded military men from victorious soldiers who wished to liquidate them. The Moors entered empty apartments, collecting rugs and silverware which they then naïvely tried to sell to neighbors in the same building. Shops were closed and shuttered. The troops

received four days of 'liberty,' after which discipline was quickly restored and the Nationalists began to administer the Catalan capital with the cooperation of most of the municipal employees. Their planes bombed the roads along which some 170,000 civilians and 300,000 defeated soldiers were fleeing to France. The League for the Rights of Man wished to cover the highways with Red Cross flags, but the IRC refused the request as a clear violation of the Geneva Convention. In any case it would have been a useless gesture; the pilots knew what and whom they were bombing.

The cabinet had retreated to Figueras, the last town of any importance on the road to France. On 4 February the Nationalists occupied Gerona. On the 6th, the leaders of the Republic – Azaña, Negrín, Luis Companys (President of the Catalan government) and José Antonio Aguirre (Basque President) – crossed the frontier together, on foot. On 8 February the victors reached Figueras, and on that same day the British navy arranged the transfer of Minorca from Republican to Nationalist authority. By this action they earned diplomatic credit with General Franco, satisfied themselves that Mussolini would not dominate the Balearics and evacuated several hundred people who would otherwise have suffered imprisonment or death. During the afternoon of 9 February the Nationalists occupied the frontier from Perthus to Port Bou, and by the 12th practically the entire border was sealed.

On 14 February the Nationalist government promulgated a decree of political responsibilities according to which all those who had opposed the *movimiento nacional* in action 'or by grave passivity' in the period since 1 October 1934 would be held accountable. The terms of the decree could be applied to any civil servant, officeholder, party or trade union leader, militiaman or soldier who had been involved in the Asturian or Catalan revolts, or in any of the activities of the Popular Front. In the impromptu refugee camps on the beaches of Argelès and Saint-Cyprien the ex-Republican soldiers debated the meaning of the decree. Nationalist officers, accompanied by French police, visited the camps and assured the men that no one would be persecuted for mere opinion or party membership. In late February and March perhaps 70,000 chose repatriation, and returned to their homeland under guard at the Hendaye–Irún border. Upwards of 400,000 military and civilian refugees remained in France. During the same weeks, in Toulouse, the Republican government split apart irreconcilably. Negrín, Del Vayo and the Communists insisted on continued resistance at least until the 250,000 soldiers in the central zone were given guarantees against political reprisal. The President of the Republic, Manuel Azaña, the President of the Cortes, Diego Martínez Barrio, and the Catalan and Basque Presidents Companys and Aguirre all opposed further resistance. General Rojo had already resigned. On 27 February France and Great Britain recognized the Nationalist government, and a few hours later President Azaña resigned his office.

Prime Minister Negrín had flown back to the central zone, where the remaining professional Generals, Matallana, Menéndez and Escobar, all told him that the Republican army could not fight on. In Madrid a non-Communist professional officer, Colonel Segismundo Casado, undertook to form a Council of National Defense which would, hopefully, be able to negotiate better surrender terms than could be obtained by Negrín. The Council included Julián Besteiro, particularly beloved by the people of Madrid both in the years when he had served as President of the Cortes and in his wartime capacity as a municipal councilor who had chosen to share the fate of the besieged city rather than go abroad as a diplomat, and General Miaja, hero of the defense of Madrid, who had joined the Communist Party but who now agreed that the war must be ended. The Council was also supported by the anarchist General Cipriano Mera, and by most anarchists and Socialists in the capital. On 5 March it seized power. Negrín, torn between his belief in continued resistance and his desire to avoid a civil war within the defeated Republican camp, did not react. The Communists in Madrid and Ciudad Real rose in the name of the 'legitimate' Negrín government, and were put down by 13 March at the cost of some 1,000 lives.

On 14 March the Nationalist Court of Political Responsibilities opened its sessions under the chairmanship of Ramón Serrano Súñer. On the Madrid radio Besteiro talked of a peace of reconciliation. Over the air waves from Saragossa came the voice of Serrano Súñer, proclaiming a peace of victory. The Casado junta was no more able than Negrín had been to extract concessions from Burgos. They were told, as the soldiers in the French camps had been told, that the authorities would be generous 'with those who, having committed no crimes, had through deception been drawn into the struggle.' They reiterated that 'neither mere service in the red forces nor having acted simply in political parties unconnected with the *movimiento nacional* would be considered motives of political responsibility.'*

On 26 March the Nationalists indicated that an advance was scheduled to begin on all fronts, that Republican troops should be sure to raise the white flag and send hostages to the Nationalist commanders. Besteiro went on the air once more to urge soldiers and civilians alike to walk out beyond the line of trenches and welcome the entering Nationalists as brothers. Burgos had indicated that it would permit the junta officials to leave Spain, and in his office in the basement of the Ministry of the Interior Besteiro urged his younger colleagues to take advantage of the opportunity. He himself had decided, with the unspoken hope of softening the fate of his compatriots, to remain in the city. The entry was delayed another twenty-four hours by the task of removing the mines which had been sown along the entire western edge of the capital more than two years previously. Even so, several civilians were injured on their way to meet the Nationalist army on 30 March.

During the days 28–31 March the Nationalists received the surrender of the Republican garrisons throughout the central and southern zones. The last motor boats and fishing vessels set sail from Valencia, some toward France, some toward North Africa. Small groups of both civilian and military refugees continued to slip across the mountainous Aragonese border. At Alicante the Italian General Gambara was prepared to permit the evacuation of political refugees waiting in the Argentine consulate. On 31 March a French cruiser appeared offshore, but turned back in view of the mined waters and the uncertain reception. The Nationalists wanted no repetition of the separate Basque surrender effort of August 1937, and so, later in the day, the Foreign Legion arrived to take over jurisdiction from Gambara. On 1 April 1939 the civil war ended with the complete and unconditional victory of General Franco.

* The cited phrases are drawn from Nationalist statements printed in *El Socialista* of Madrid, 28 March 1939.

The Valley of the Fallen, a memorial – built in the typically massive, unimaginative style of twentieth-century dictatorships – theoretically intended to honor the half million dead of both camps, and containing the eventual resting-place of the Caudillo.

Chapter Ten

THE CIVIL WAR IN PERSPECTIVE

Each year on 1 April the Spanish government celebrates the anniversary of victory in what it variously calls the 'Crusade' and the 'War of Liberation' (from Communism). In its desire to impress upon the people the high cost of the war it habitually refers to *un millón de muertos*, one million deaths, among a population which in 1936 totaled somewhat over 25,000,000. As of mid-1939 Spain had indeed lost about 1,000,000 people, since about 400,000 had emigrated as political refugees, most of whom did not return home until after the Second World War. Deaths attributable directly to the war and its political aftermath total about 300,000 to 400,000, and it is the manner of those deaths which has burned itself into the agonized, if largely silent, consciousness of the Spanish people. The sum of

General Franco takes the salute at the 1960 parade celebrating the anniversary of the end of the Civil War.

battle deaths is relatively low, 100,000 to 150,000, principally because, even though the war lasted thirty-two months, there were long lulls in the fighting. But the proportion of *deaths* among total *casualties* in each major battle is very high, due to the incomplete training and the combative ardor of the troops. Most horrible is the fact that executions and reprisal killings were far and away the largest single category of deaths. On the Republican side there were about 20,000 such, committed mostly during the first three months of the struggle. The Nationalists, counting the entire time from July 1936 to the end of mass executions in 1944, liquidated 150,000 to 200,000 of their compatriots, on a scale of violence comparable to the repression of the Paris Commune in 1871, the Nazi repressions in eastern Europe and Yugoslavia, the Columbian Civil War following the assassination of Jorge Eliécer Gaitán in 1948, the slaughter of the Indonesian Communists in 1965 and the Nigerian Civil War of 1970.

The sheer ferocity of the Spanish Civil War and its aftermath can only be understood in terms of the intense ideological commitments which it aroused. For the Nationalists who rose in military rebellion, it was an anti-Communist, anti-atheist and anti-liberal crusade. In their view Catholic Spain had been poisoned by every doctrine emanating from the French and Russian Revolutions: by secular liberalism, parliamentarism, international Masonry, Marxism and Bolshevism. For the mass of peasants and workingmen who spontaneously rushed to defend the Republic it was a revolution, a long-awaited opportunity to create a decentralized, egalitarian, collectivist society based on a combination of Marxist and anarchist principles, and, at an intuitive level, fulfilling a deeply religious people's conception of what Christianity should really mean. For the Republicans and parliamentary Socialists, and for majority public opinion in the Western countries, it was a crusade to save Spain, and Europe, from Fascism, in particular from that most aggressive, nihilistic and barbaric form of Fascism embodied in the Hitler régime. These ideological commitments help to explain the extraordinary self-sacrifices and the reckless bravery on both sides. They help to explain also the spontaneous terrorism in both zones during the first few months. They explain in part the cold terror methodically exercised in the Nationalist area throughout the war, and the selective terror of both the Communists and their enemies on the far Left in the Republican zone.

Until the siege of Madrid the war seemed to most Spaniards to be primarily a Spanish affair. Not that they were unaware of foreign intervention, but motives both of political pride and of spiritual commitment prevented them from facing squarely the extent of foreign involvement. Those in authority knew that German-Italian-Portuguese aid had prevented the failure of the *pronunciamiento* in late July. Everyone knew that Russian tanks and planes, and the International Brigades, had been indispensable in halting the

DIE FREIHEIT KÄMPFT IN IHREN REIHEN

Nach Delacroix

Freedom fights in their ranks. Photomontage by John Heartfield after Delacroix's *Liberty Guiding the People* (1831)

Nationalist advance at Madrid. Throughout the rest of the war it was clear that the outcome of each major battle, and the outcome of the war as a whole, would depend on which side could obtain the greater quantity and quality of foreign supplies, exception made for the fact that the Republicans were not nearly so dependent on foreign personnel as were the Nationalists.

By late 1937 the people of both zones were war-weary. The destructiveness of modern weapons had come as a surprise even to Spanish military men. In terms of artillery bombardment and slogging trench warfare Spain had not lived through anything resembling the United States Civil War or the First World War. The Spaniards' image of war in 1936 was of short infantry encounters involving small units and only incidentally affecting civilian life – as in the Carlist and Moroccan wars. After Madrid and Guernica they knew the meaning of modern artillery barrages and air raids. They were also disillusioned by pervasive foreign influence far from the battle-front. In the Nationalist zone Moors and Italians were omnipresent. The Germans were less numerous but the Falangist press, aping the Nazis, printed anti-Semitic drivel which had rarely been heard in Spain since the seventeenth century. The best hotels were reserved for German officers, and Germany was pressing for important economic concessions as the price of her fraternal aid. In the Republican zone Comintern agents controlled the flow of Soviet supplies to the army and privately liquidated anti-Stalinist elements among both Spaniards and the International Brigades. It was humiliating and morally corrosive to have Stalin's paranoia exercising constant influence in Republican politics. With each passing month the population in both zones tended to become increasingly xenophobic, while at the same time the two governments became increasingly dependent upon their foreign allies.

From an international perspective the victory of the Spanish Nationalists was a further triumph for Fascism. Since 1933 the small central and eastern European nations had adopted some form of right-wing dictatorship and had largely reoriented their political and economic policies toward collaboration with the Axis. Czechoslovakia, which had tried to resist this trend, had been destroyed by Hitler. Now Spain would be added to the political-economic orbit of the Axis. Triumph for Fascism was conversely a defeat for both Western democracy and Communism. The Western failure to support the Spanish Republic from 1936 to 1939, coupled with the failure to help the Czechoslovak Republic defend itself against Hitler in 1938, created a feeling of moral apathy, not to say cynicism. When Hitler launched the Second World War, six months after the final destruction of the Spanish and Czech democracies, few of the young men mobilized in the West could feel that any great moral cause was at stake; they were simply getting ready to defend their own countries after having sacrificed their best available allies and their democratic principles. As for the Soviet Union, it had temporarily saved its own skin by signing a Non-Aggression Pact with Germany.

Within Spain, victory and iron will enabled General Franco substantially to fulfil the aims of the anti-Communist and anti-liberal crusade. All the political organizations of the Republican era, and the two great trade union federations, Socialist and anarchist, were proscribed. A controlled press was able to prevent the dissemination of Marxist, anarchist, atheist and internationalist ideas. All Republican legislation on regional autonomy, separation of Church and state, land reform and divorce was abrogated. For five years prior to the Civil War Spain had been a mildly reformist, unstable, parliamentary Republic. After the Civil War it was a conservative military dictatorship, and that dictatorship became, through the cruelty, the skill and the longevity of General Franco, the most powerful single Spanish government since the reign of Philip II in the sixteenth

Opposite: Crush Fascism. Anonymous Spanish photomontage.

AIXAFEM EL FEIXISME

century. The régime was consolidated by roughly eight years of political proscription (1936–44) positively awe-inspiring in its lack of pity and lack of imagination. It was as if the victors had deliberately set themselves not to reconcile the defeated majority of their compatriots. The pacifist–Socialist Julián Besteiro died in prison in 1940. The President of the Generalitat who had done everything possible in 1936 to reduce terrorism and to help threatened political opponents escape abroad, Luis Companys, was returned to Spain by the Gestapo and shot. Tens of thousands of veterans, who desired nothing so much as to forget politics and rebuild their shattered country, were court-martialed and either shot or given twenty- and thirty-year prison terms. While awaiting death or serving their time they could perform forced labor and attend involuntary religious instruction. Mass executions ended in 1944 (with the approaching defeat of the Fascist powers) and amnesties were increasingly granted during the 1950s.

Since the early 1950s several factors have mitigated the harshness of the régime: the economic benefits from European trade, investment and tourism; the example of unprecedented West European prosperity, particularly the fact that postwar Italy and West Germany have flourished under parliamentary régimes; the employment opportunities in Western Europe for Spanish workers, especially in such formerly 'decadent democracies' as France; and the considerable measure of industrialization taking place with the help of West European and American capital. The continuing absence of political liberty means that after thirty years an entire generation has grown up without any experience in the arts of constitutional government which Spaniards had only begun to learn in the period from 1876 to 1936. On the other hand, Spain today can reasonably hope to avoid the two great problems (land reform and aggressive Fascism) which destroyed the Republic in 1936: the former (which has never been implemented) is no longer so pressing a problem because of increasing industrialization; and the whole experience of Europe since 1945 makes it most unlikely that boastful, aggressive, nihilistic Fascism will again triumph.

Ever since 1945 Spaniards of all persuasions have been saying that there must never be another Civil War (a sentiment which has also contributed to the longevity of the Franco régime). It is impossible for anyone to foresee what a given historical experience will mean to people in the perspective of the long future. But as an American I know that even after a full century, and without there having been a proscription remotely comparable to that which occurred in Spain, the United States has by no means fully resolved the issues which caused the Civil War of 1861–65. I am convinced also, though I cannot prove it quantitatively, that a higher proportion of the Spanish population felt emotionally and politically committed in 1936 than was the case in the America of 1776, the France of 1789, the Central Europe of 1848 or the Russia of 1917. From 1931 to 1939 the Spanish

Two Carlist soldiers mount guard over the shrine of the Virgin of Pilar, patroness of the Nationalist forces.

people lived through a uniquely intense experience of reform, revolution and counter-revolution, civil war and international intervention. Those who led the Republic earned the right to feel that they (building on the example of liberal educators and statesmen since the 1870s) had done more to improve the quality of life in Spain than any governing group since the time of Charles III in the eighteenth century. Those who supported revolutionary collectivist experiments felt that they were offering not only to Spain but to the world an example of social organization superior to that of either Western democratic capitalism or Soviet Communism. Those who supported the Insurgent generals felt that they were rescuing Spain for the Holy Roman Apostolic religion, and from disorder and atheist Bolshevism. In that cauldron of conflicting ideals how can one measure the extent of sacrifices and illusions, the acts of nobility and terror? By what right, and from what reserves of passion and energy, did Francisco Franco and Juan Negrín bear out the lives of their countrymen, even to the edge of doom? Who were the most authentic Spaniards, the humane compromisers like Azaña, Besteiro, Companys and ultimately both Prieto and Largo Caballero? Or those who, according to the metaphor of 'La Pasionaria,' chose to die on their feet rather than to live on their knees? Or those who fought to restore a traditionalist society inspired by the examples of Ferdinand and Isabella, and of the Catholic Counter-Reformation? When questions of diplomatic blackmail, foreign armament, financial backing, specific laws and political organization will all have become pluperfect tense, the people of Spain will still debate the spiritual dilemmas of the Civil War and will still wrestle with its legacy of unresolved religious and social struggles. Hopefully they will also draw that solace which men, ever since the ancient Greeks, have drawn from the grandeur of tragic experience.

Xavier Bueno, *In Memory of My Friend* (1938).

BIBLIOGRAPHY

In preparing this brief bibliography I have kept the following objectives in mind: to list books in English unless the only serious, authoritative treatment of the topic is in a foreign language; in any case to list books which are readily available in English and American libraries; to concentrate on those aspects of the subject which I have emphasized in the text.

Annotated bibliographies are found in Burnett Bolloten, *The Grand Camouflage* (London: Hollis and Carter, 1961; New York: Praeger, 1961), which deals principally with non-Stalinist revolution and Communist Party influence; an expanded, still more thoroughly documented study of the same topics by the same author is *The Spanish Revolution: The Left and the Struggle for Power during the Civil War* (Chapel Hill, University of North Carolina Press, 1978); P. Broué and E. Témime, *La Révolution et la guerre d'Espagne* (Paris: Éditions de Minuit, 1961), Eng. edition Faber and Faber for the Massachusetts Institute of Technology Press, 1972; Gabriel Jackson, *The Spanish Republic and the Civil War* (Princeton University Press, 1965); Stanley G. Payne, *The Spanish Revolution* (London: Weidenfeld and Nicolson, 1970; New York: Norton, 1970); and Herbert R. Southworth, *La Guerra civil Espanola y sus consecuencias, 1936–1972, una bibliografía* (Paris: Ruedo Ibérico, 1973). Very comprehensive listings, including some pamphlets, are found in Ricardo de la Cierva, *Bibliografía general sobre la guerra de Espana y sus antecedentes históricos* (Barcelona, 1968), and Hugh Thomas, *The Spanish Civil War* (London: Eyre and Spottiswoode, 1961; New York: Harper and Row, 1961). The several 1960s editions of Thomas were factually unreliable; the third edition, 1977, is by far the best.

Most valuable for background and historical perspective are Gerald Brenan, *The Spanish Labyrinth* (Cambridge University Press, 1950); Raymond Carr, *Spain 1808–1939* (Oxford: Clarendon Press, 1966), and Raymond Carr, ed., *The Republic and the Civil War in Spain* (London: Macmillan, 1971). Gerald Meaker, *The Revolutionary Left in Spain, 1914–1923* (Stanford University Press, 1974), is indispensable for understanding the early political experience of the Left leaders of the 1930s. Shlomo Ben-Ami, *The Origins of the Second Republic in Spain* (Oxford University Press, 1978), details the internal breakdown of the Primo de Rivera dictatorship. Angel Viñas, *La Alemania Nazi y el 18 de Julio* (revised ed. Alianza Editorial, 1977), analyzes German diplomatic, economic, and military interest in Spain from c. 1914 to 1936. Paul Preston, *The Coming of the Spanish Civil War* (London: Macmillan, and New York: Barnes and Noble, 1978), illustrates the counterpoint between Rightist intransigence and Socialist disunity. The political history of the Right during the Republic is ably covered in Richard A. H. Robinson, *The Origins of Franco's Spain* (Newton Abbot: David and Charles, 1970). On the regional movements there are two important books by Maximiano García Venero, *Historia del nacionalismo catalan* (Madrid, 1944) and *Historia del nacionalismo vasco* (Madrid, 1945). Concerning the land problem, Edward M. Malefakis, *Agrarian Reform and Peasant Revolution in Spain* (Yale University Press, 1970), is unique in its thorough analysis. On the Church and social questions, Joan Connelly, *The Tragic Week* (Harvard University Press, 1968), gives the most accurate account of the anticlerical riots of 1909, and Alfredo Mendizábal, *The Martyrdom of Spain* (London: Geoffrey Bles, 1938; New York: Scribner's, 1937), discusses the anticlericalism of the 1930s from the viewpoint of a liberal Catholic professor of law. The background of the army is summarized in S. G. Payne, *Politics and the Military in Modern Spain* (Stanford University Press, 1967). For a paranoid history, factually unreliable but significant for the thinking of ruling military and police circles, Eduardo Comín Colomer, *Historia secreta de la segunda república* (Madrid, 1954–55).

The finest English-language treatment of any military aspect is Robert G. Colodny, *The Struggle for Madrid* (New York: Paine Whitman, 1958). The best general accounts in Spanish, albeit victors' versions, are Manuel Aznar, *Historia militar de la guerra de España* (Madrid, several editions since 1940 with little textual revision, though the three-volume edition published by Editora Nacional between 1958 and 1963 is rich in illustrations), and Luis María de Lojendio, *Operaciones militares de la guerra de España* (Barcelona: Montaner y Simon, 1940), which has especially fine maps. José Martín Blázquez, *I Helped Build an Army* (London: Secker and Warburg, 1939); several works by the former chief-of-staff, General Vicente Rojo – *¡ Alerta los pueblos!* (Buenos Aires, 1939), *¡ España Heroica!* (Buenos Aires, 1942) and *Así fué la defensa de Madrid* (Mexico: Era 1967) – and Julián Henríquez Caubín, *La batalla del Ebro* (Mexico D.F., 1949), all deal with the war experience in the Republican zone. José María Iribarren, *Con el General Mola* (Saragossa, 1937), Benito Gómez Oliveiros, *General Moscardó* (Barcelona, 1956), and Alfredo Kindelán, *Mis cuadernos de guerra* (Madrid, 1945), illustrate the Nationalist war experience. J. Salas Larrazabal, *La guerra de España desde el aire* (Barcelona: Ariel, 1969), has much important information from the military archives but also uses questionable statistics uncritically. G.L. Steer, *The Tree of Gernika* (London: Hodder and Stoughton, 1938), is an eyewitness account of the Basque campaign, and Herbert R. Southworth, *Guernica! Guernica!* (University of California Press, 1977), shows the extraordinary efforts made by both the French press and the Nationalist authorities to hide the truth concerning the bombing. H.L. Matthews, *Two Wars and More to Come* (New York: Carrick and Evans, 1938), has frontline observations of the Quinto-Belchite operations. Three Swiss war correspondents were intelligent observers of military action and morale: Eddy Bauer, *Rouge et Or* (Neuchâtel: Victor Attinger, 1938), Georges Oudard, *Chemises noires, brunes, vertes en Espagne* (Paris, 1938), and O. Treyvaud, *Les deux Espagnes* (Lausanne, 1937). Of the many war memoirs published in Spain since the end of the Franco era, most outstanding is Manuel Tagüena Lacorte, *Testimonio de Dos Guerras* (Barcelona, Planeta, 1978).

On the internal history of the Republican zone, Frank Borkenau, *The Spanish Cockpit* (London: Faber and Faber, 1937), H.E. Kaminski, *Ceux de Barcelone* (Barcelona: Tierra y Libertad, 1938), and Agustín Souchy, *Entre los campesinos de Aragon* (Barcelona: Tierra y Libertad, 1938), all contain valuable observations of anarchist collectives, revolutionary politics and violence. Important English-language works concerning the Anarchists are Robert W. Kern, *Red Years/Black Years: A Political History of Spanish Anarchism, 1911–1937* (Philadelphia: The Institute for the Study of Human Issues, 1978); Murray Bookchin, *The Spanish Anarchists* (New York: Free Life Editions, 1977); and Sam Dolgoff, *The Anarchist Collectives* (New York: Free Life Editions, 1974). David T. Cattell, *Communism and the Spanish Civil War* (University of California Press, 1955), analyzes the astonishing growth and influence of the party. George Orwell, *Homage to Catalonia* (London: Secker and Warburg, 1938), gives a vivid portrait of the non-Stalinist Left and a masterly analysis of newspaper propaganda; Julián Zugazagoitia, *Historia de la guerra de España* (Buenos Aires, 1940, reissued under the title *Guerra y vicisitudes de los españoles*, Paris: Librarie Espagnole, 1968, and again in Barcelona, Editorial Crítica, Grijalbo, 1978), is invaluable for insight into Republican-zone politics. The author was editor of *El Socialista* and a cabinet colleague of Prieto and Negrín. The much mythologized fate of the Spanish gold reserve has been accurately chronicled in Angel Viñas, *El Oro Español en la Guerra civil* (Madrid: Instituto de Estudios Fiscales, 1976).

On the internal history of the Nationalist zone there are two readable but factually undependable biographies: Brian Crozier, *Franco* (London: Eyre and Spottiswoode, 1967), and George Hills, *Franco: the Man and His Nation* (London: Robert Hale, 1967). A completely dependable, concise synthesis is J.W.D. Trythall, *Franco* (London: Hart-Davis, 1970). S.G. Payne, *Falange* (Stanford University Press, 1962), is a party history based both on documents and on interviews. Martin Blinkhorn, *Carlism and Crisis in Spain, 1931–1939* (Cambridge University Press, 1975), distinguishes the Carlist role within the Spanish Right. M. García Venero, *La Falange en la guerra de España* (Paris: Ruedo Ibérico, 1967), defends the role of Hedilla and should be read along with the critical commentary by H.R. Southworth, *Antifalange* (Paris: Ruedo Ibérico, 1967). Ramón Serrano Súñer, *Entre Hendaya y Gibraltar* (Madrid, 1947), is the political autobiography of Franco's brother-in-law and close adviser.

Concerning Nationalist terror, Georges Bernanos, *Les Grands Cimetières sous la lune* (Paris, 1938, a shortened form of which was published in London in the same year by Boriswood under the title *A Diary of My Times*), is a Catholic's personal testimonial of the purge in Majorca. Antonio Ruiz Vilaplana, *Burgos Justice* (London: Constable, 1938; New York: Knopf, 1938), is the work of a Spanish municipal official, Marino Ayerra Redín, *No me avergoncé del evangelio* (Buenos Aires: Peripolo, 1959), is the testimony of a Basque priest. Ian Gibson, *The Death of Lorca* (London and New York: W.H. Allen, 1973), is a model of accurate documentation. Gabriel Avilés, *Tribunales rojos* (Barcelona, 1939), expounds Communist terror as known to a liberal Barcelona lawyer, and Julián Gorkin, *Canibales políticos* (Mexico D.F.: Quetzal, 1941), has a wealth of detail about Stalinist persecution of the non-Stalinist Left. Jesús de Galíndez, *Los vascos en el Madrid sitiado* (Buenos Aires, 1945), is rich in information on anarchist terror, prison raids and the situation in the foreign embassies. Gabriel Jackson, *Historian's Quest* (New York: Knopf, 1969), contains testimonials on wartime and postwar repression.

Accurate and well-documented on different aspects of foreign intervention are: David T. Cattell, *Soviet Diplomacy and the Spanish Civil War* (University of California Press, 1957); Emilio Faldella, *Venti mesi di guerra in Spagna* (Florence, 1939); John F. Coverdale, *Italian Intervention in the Spanish Civil War* (Princeton University Press, 1975); Glenn T. Harper, *German Economic Policy in Spain* (The Hague: Mouton, 1967); Manfred Merkes, *Die deutsche Politik gegenüber dem spanischen Bürgerkrieg, 1936–1939* (Bonn: Röhrscheid, 1961); Dante Puzzo, *Spain and the Great Powers, 1936–1941* (Columbia University Press, 1962); Richard P. Traina, *American Diplomacy and the Spanish Civil War* (University of Indiana Press, 1968); Norman J. Padelford, *International Law and Diplomacy in the Spanish Civil Strife* (New York, 1939). Marcel Junod, *Warrior without Weapons* (London: Cape, 1951), is particularly concerned with the role of the International Red Cross. The sections on Spain by Katharine Duff in the Royal Institute for International Affairs' *Survey of International Affairs* for 1937 and 1938 (London: Oxford University Press, 1938 and 1939) remain among the best English-language accounts.

An excellent personal memoir of the International Brigades is Alvah Bessie, *Men in Battle* (New York: Scribner's, 1939). Ludwig Renn, *Der spanische Krieg* (Berlin, 1956), has notable maps and military analysis; the author was a former German imperial officer. A fine general account of both the politics and the actions of the brigades is Jacques Delperrie de Bayac, *Les Brigades internationales* (Paris: Fayard, 1968). For the concerns of the American intellectual community see Allen Guttman, *The Wound in the Heart* (New York: Free Press of Glencoe, 1962). Peter Stansky and William Abrahams, *Journey to the Frontier* (London: Constable, 1966; Boston: Little Brown, 1966), is a joint biography of two young English intellectuals, John Cornford and Julian Bell, who died in Spain. Pietro Nenni, *Spagna* (Milan: Avanti, 1958), is the memoir of the Italian Left-Socialist leader; a French translation has been published as *La Guerre d'Espagne* (Paris: Maspero, 1960). Magnificent oral testimonies from all classes and parties to the Civil War have been collected and edited by Ronald Fraser, *Blood of Spain: An Oral History of the Spanish Civil War* (New York: Pantheon Press, 1979). Among the many novels, Ernest Hemingway, *For Whom the Bell Tolls* (New York: Scribner's, 1940; London: Cape, 1941), illuminates the motives of both Spanish guerrillas and Internationals. André Malraux's novel *L'Espoir*, published in Great Britain as *Days of Hope* (London: Routledge, 1938) and in America as *Man's Hope* (New York: Random House, 1938), gives vivid, quasi-documentary accounts of the leftist militia in the first weeks. Gustav Regler, *The Great Crusade* (New York: Longmans, 1940), epitomizes the hopes of the German and Italian anti-Fascist volunteers. Ramón Sender, in *Seven Red Sundays* (London: Faber and Faber, 1936) and in many later novels and stories, interprets the war as a Spanish left-liberal. José Gironella, in *The Cypresses Believe in God* (New York: Knopf, 1956) and in *One Million Dead* (New York: Knopf, 1963), portrays the war from a conservative, disabused viewpoint. Finally, an indispensable work for understanding the intense passion and propaganda intent of most Civil War literature is Herbert R. Southworth, *El mito de la cruzada de Franco* (Paris: Ruedo Ibérico, 1963); French translation as *Le Mythe de la croisade de Franco* (1964).

LIST OF ILLUSTRATIONS

INDEX

Page numbers in italics refer to illustrations